True Facts That Sound Like Bullshit:
Human Stupidity & Failures
A Journey Through Humanity's Most Spectacular Mistakes

Table of Contents

True Facts That Sound Like Bullshit: Human Stupidity & Failures
A Journey Through Humanity's Most Spectacular Mistakes

Chapter 1: Epic Fails Through History

History is written by the winners, they say. But what about the spectacular losers? The kings who burned down their own kingdoms, the generals who forgot which way was forward, and the empires that collapsed because someone couldn't read a map? Welcome to the hall of fame of human stupidity, where common sense went to die and logic never got an invitation to the party.

The thing about epic historical fails is that they often start with the most reasonable intentions. Nobody wakes up thinking, "Today I shall destroy civilization as we know it." Yet somehow, through a delightful combination of hubris, ignorance, and sheer bloody-mindedness, humans have managed to turn the simplest tasks into catastrophic disasters that would make a Greek tragedy seem like a light comedy.

1. The King Who Burned His Own Kingdom Over a Rumor

In 1814, Crown Prince Regent Christian Frederick of Denmark-Norway found himself in quite the pickle. Napoleon had been defeated, and the Treaty of Kiel had awarded Norway to Sweden. Rather than accepting this diplomatic reality like a reasonable person, Christian Frederick decided he'd rather burn his entire kingdom to the ground than hand it over to his Swedish neighbors.

What started as a rumor about Swedish troops massing at the border quickly spiraled into full-scale paranoia. Christian Frederick ordered the destruction of all major infrastructure—bridges, roads, government buildings—anything that might be useful to an occupying force. The problem was, there was no occupying force. The Swedes were still negotiating terms and had no immediate plans for invasion. By the time cooler heads prevailed, Norway had essentially demolished itself for absolutely no reason.

But Christian Frederick wasn't done yet. When he finally realized his mistake, rather than admitting error, he doubled down. He declared Norwegian independence and drafted a constitution, knowing full well this would provoke the very war he was trying to avoid. The resulting conflict lasted several months, cost thousands of lives, and ended exactly where it would have if he'd just accepted the original treaty terms in the first place.

The crown prince's spectacular miscalculation perfectly illustrates what psychologists now call the "sunk cost fallacy"—the tendency to continue a course of action simply because you've already invested so much in it, even when that course is clearly doomed. Christian Frederick had burned so many bridges (literally and figuratively) that admitting error seemed more costly than continuing down the path of destruction.

Perhaps most remarkably, contemporary accounts suggest that Christian Frederick never fully understood why his approach was problematic. In letters to his advisors, he expressed genuine bewilderment that other European powers didn't support his "principled stand" against Swedish aggression that existed primarily in his own imagination.

The story would be hilarious if it weren't for the thousands of Norwegian peasants who starved that winter because their prince had destroyed the infrastructure needed to transport food and supplies. Sometimes the cost of royal stupidity is measured not in gold or territory, but in human lives—a lesson that seems to require relearning in every generation.

2. Wars Started by Animals

If you think human conflicts are irrational, wait until you hear about the wars triggered by livestock, confused cavalry horses, and one particularly aggressive pig. The animal kingdom has been inadvertently shaping human military history for millennia, usually with results that would be comedic if they weren't so deadly.

The Pig War of 1859 between the United States and Britain began when an American farmer shot a British pig that was rooting through his potato garden on San Juan Island. This porcine trespass escalated into a months-long military standoff involving warships, hundreds of troops, and heated diplomatic exchanges between London and Washington. The pig, having already paid the ultimate price for its agricultural crimes, was presumably unaware that it had nearly triggered an international conflict.

What makes this even more absurd is that both sides knew the dispute was ridiculous, but neither could back down without losing face. American General William S. Harney dispatched Captain George Pickett (yes, of Pickett's Charge fame) with 64 soldiers to protect American interests on the island. The British responded by sending three warships with 461 marines. For months, hundreds of armed men glared at each other across pig-free potato gardens, probably wondering how their careers had reached this point.

The situation reached peak absurdity when British Admiral Robert L. Baynes refused orders from the colonial governor to forcibly remove the Americans, reportedly saying he would not "involve two great nations in a war over a squabble about a pig." The crisis was eventually resolved through diplomacy, with both sides maintaining token forces on the island until 1872, when the matter was settled by international arbitration. The pig remained dead throughout these proceedings.

Even more bizarre was the War of Jenkins' Ear (1739-1748), which began when Spanish coast guards allegedly cut off the ear of British captain Robert Jenkins during a search of his ship. When Jenkins preserved his severed ear in a jar and presented it to Parliament seven years later, it provided the perfect excuse for a war that politicians had been wanting anyway. Whether the ear was actually Jenkins' own, or indeed whether it had ever been attached to anyone at all, remains a matter of historical debate.

The most militarily significant animal-triggered disaster occurred during World War I, when a flock of sheep wandered onto a battlefield during the Battle of Verdun. Artillery observers, mistaking the moving white shapes for advancing German troops in winter camouflage, called down a massive bombardment on their own positions. The resulting chaos allowed actual German forces to advance several kilometers before the mistake was discovered. The sheep, like most animals in military history, were entirely innocent of any strategic intentions.

These incidents reveal something profound about human nature: our desperate need to find meaning and purpose in random events. A pig eating potatoes becomes a matter of national sovereignty. A flock of sheep becomes evidence of enemy advancement. We're so convinced that everything happens for a reason that we'll manufacture reasons even when the only explanation is coincidence and bad luck.

3. The Dumbest Battle Decisions in History

Military history is littered with brilliant strategies and tactical masterstrokes. It's also absolutely stuffed with decisions so breathtakingly stupid that they've become case studies in what not to do. The remarkable thing isn't that these mistakes happened—it's that they were made by professional soldiers who should have known better.

The Charge of the Light Brigade at Balaclava in 1854 has become the poster child for military incompetence, immortalized by Tennyson's poem about noble soldiers riding into certain death. What the poem doesn't capture is the staggering cascade of miscommunication that made the disaster inevitable. Lord Raglan, observing from a hilltop, could see Russian forces removing guns from some captured positions. He sent a vaguely worded order to attack "the guns," not realizing that from the valley floor, his subordinates could only see the main Russian artillery battery.

Captain Edward Nolan, carrying the message, had his own interpretation of what should be attacked. When questioned by Lord Lucan about which guns were meant, Nolan pointed dramatically toward the Russian battery and shouted something that was lost in the wind. The Light Brigade, already frustrated by weeks of inaction, saw an opportunity for glory and charged directly into the concentrated firepower of an entire artillery position.

The result was predictable: nearly 300 casualties in minutes, the destruction of Britain's finest cavalry unit, and a lesson in the importance of clear communication that military academies still teach today. What makes it even more tragic is that multiple officers had opportunities to question or clarify the orders, but the rigid hierarchy of Victorian military command made such questioning unthinkable.

Even more spectacular was General Custer's decision-making at Little Bighorn in 1876. Despite being warned by his Native American scouts that the enemy encampment was the largest they'd ever seen, Custer dismissed their concerns and divided his already outnumbered force into three separate groups. His rationale seems to have been that the enemy would flee if given time, so a immediate attack was necessary to prevent their escape.

This logic might have made sense if Custer had been facing a small band of raiders, but he was actually confronting one of the largest gatherings of Plains tribes in American history—somewhere between 1,800 and 2,500 warriors. Rather than fleeing, they were perfectly prepared to fight and had chosen their ground carefully. Custer's 210 men were annihilated, not because they lacked courage, but because their commander had made every possible tactical error in sequence.

The common thread in these military disasters is overconfidence combined with poor information processing. Custer ignored intelligence that contradicted his preconceptions. The officers at Balaclava assumed their orders made sense rather than seeking clarification. In both cases, the cognitive bias known as confirmation bias—the tendency to interpret information in ways that support existing beliefs—proved literally fatal.

What's particularly maddening about these failures is that they were often preventable with just a moment's reflection. A single question—"Are you sure about those numbers?" or "Which guns exactly?"—might have changed history. But asking questions implies uncertainty, and military culture has traditionally valued decisive action over careful deliberation, even when that decisiveness leads straight off a cliff.

4. When Inventions Outran Human Sense

The relationship between human ingenuity and human wisdom has always been a bit strained. We're remarkably good at figuring out how to do things, and remarkably bad at figuring out whether we should do them. History is full of inventors who created something amazing and then watched in horror as humanity found the most destructive possible use for it.

Take Thomas Midgley Jr., who has the dubious distinction of being called "the one human responsible for more deaths than any other single person in history." Midgley didn't set out to destroy the planet—quite the opposite. In the 1920s, he solved two major problems that were plaguing modern life. Car engines were knocking, so he invented leaded gasoline. Refrigerators were using toxic ammonia, so he developed chlorofluorocarbons (CFCs) as a safer alternative.

Both inventions were hailed as brilliant solutions to real problems. Leaded gasoline eliminated engine knock and improved performance. CFCs were non-toxic, non-flammable, and worked perfectly in refrigeration systems. Midgley was celebrated as a genius, awarded medals by scientific societies, and made wealthy by his innovations. There was just one tiny problem: both inventions turned out to be environmental disasters on a global scale.

Lead in gasoline poisoned entire generations, causing learning disabilities, behavioral problems, and reduced IQ across populations worldwide. CFCs, released into the atmosphere, began destroying the ozone layer that protects Earth from harmful radiation. Midgley lived long enough to see the evidence mounting against his creations, and reportedly spent his final years deeply troubled by the unintended consequences of his genius.

The irony reached its peak when Midgley, paralyzed by polio in his later years, invented an elaborate pulley system to help himself get in and out of bed. True to form, the contraption malfunctioned and strangled him in 1944. Even his final invention turned against him, as if the universe were making a point about the dangers of over-engineering solutions to simple problems.

Robert Oppenheimer had a similar experience with the atomic bomb. The Manhattan Project brought together the finest scientific minds of the era to solve what they saw as an urgent military problem: ending World War II as quickly as possible. The physics was fascinating, the engineering challenges were immense, and the sense of patriotic duty was overwhelming. It wasn't until Oppenheimer watched the first test explosion in the New Mexico desert that the full implications hit him.

"Now I am become Death, destroyer of worlds," he reportedly said, quoting the Bhagavad Gita. The brilliant physicist who had spent years perfecting the ultimate weapon suddenly realized he had created something that could end human civilization. Unlike Midgley, who discovered his mistakes gradually, Oppenheimer's moment of clarity came in a blinding flash that lit up the pre-dawn sky.

What these stories reveal is the fundamental problem with human innovation: we're much better at solving technical problems than at predicting social consequences. Give us a challenge—engine knock, refrigerant toxicity, military deadlock—and we'll engineer a solution. Ask us to predict how that solution will affect human behavior, social structures, or global systems over decades, and we're basically throwing darts in the dark.

The pattern keeps repeating because we're wired to focus on immediate, concrete problems rather than distant, abstract consequences. It's the same cognitive bias that makes us save money for vacation while ignoring retirement planning, or worry about plane crashes while texting and driving. Our brains are designed for solving the problems in front of us, not the problems our solutions might create.

5. Empires That Fell Because of Simple Mistakes

The fall of great empires usually gets attributed to grand historical forces—economic decline, military pressure, social upheaval. But sometimes civilizations collapse because someone forgot to carry the one, misunderstood a message, or made a clerical error that cascaded into catastrophe. These aren't the dramatic endings that make it into epic movies; they're the bureaucratic fumbles that prove even empires can die of paperwork.

The Maya civilization provides a perfect example of how administrative incompetence can doom an entire culture. Recent archaeological evidence suggests that the Classic Maya collapse around 900 CE wasn't caused by drought, warfare, or disease, but by a series of miscommunications between city-states about resource allocation during a period of climate stress. Local administrators, working with incomplete information and contradictory directives from regional capitals, made decisions that individually seemed reasonable but collectively created a cascade of supply chain failures.

The system broke down something like this: City A, experiencing crop shortages, requested grain from City B. City B, which had also heard rumors of shortages, decided to hoard its surplus rather than share it. City C, seeing that B was hoarding, began hoarding as well. Within a season, the entire trade network had seized up, not because there wasn't enough food, but because nobody trusted anyone else to share fairly. The Maya had created a prisoner's dilemma on a civilizational scale, and predictably, everyone defected.

What makes this even more tragic is that Maya record-keeping was sophisticated enough that administrators could have coordinated their response if they'd chosen to share information accurately. Instead, each city-state submitted reports that inflated their needs and understated their resources, hoping to secure better terms in negotiations. The result was a planning system based entirely on lies, which is roughly as effective as it sounds.

The Western Roman Empire's final collapse in 476 CE followed a similar pattern of administrative breakdown, though it took several centuries to fully play out. The empire had grown too large for its communication systems, creating a lag between central decisions and local implementation that made coherent policy impossible. By the 5th century, Roman bureaucrats in Gaul were still receiving directives about problems that had been solved (or had solved themselves) months earlier.

The final straw came when Emperor Julius Nepos, ruling from Dalmatia, appointed Orestes as commander of the Western Roman army without checking whether Orestes actually controlled any troops. Orestes, realizing he could act with impunity, deposed Nepos and installed his own son Romulus Augustus as emperor. When Germanic chieftain Odoacer decided to eliminate this puppet government, there was literally nobody in Rome with the authority to stop him, because the chain of command had become so tangled that no one knew who was supposed to be in charge of what.

The Byzantine Empire lasted another thousand years largely because it learned from Rome's mistakes and developed more robust systems for managing information flow across vast distances. They created redundant communication channels, standardized reporting procedures, and built in verification systems that made it harder for local officials to simply lie about their situations. It's a rare example of humans actually learning from administrative failure, which might explain why it took the Ottomans until 1453 to finally finish them off.

These imperial collapses share a common thread: they weren't caused by external enemies or natural disasters, but by the breakdown of the information systems that held complex societies together. When administrators can't trust the data they're receiving, when communication delays make coordination impossible, and when the incentives for accurate reporting are overwhelmed by incentives for self-preservation, even the mightiest empire becomes just a collection of confused people making contradictory decisions.

The lesson here isn't that empires are fragile—it's that complexity requires competence. The more moving parts a system has, the more ways it can break down, and the more important it becomes to have people who actually understand how those parts work together. When you combine imperial ambitions with bureaucratic incompetence, you get some of history's most expensive mistakes.

Chapter 2: When Science Went Wrong

Science is supposed to be humanity's most reliable method for figuring out how the world works. It's based on careful observation, rigorous testing, and the revolutionary idea that we should believe evidence over authority. In practice, however, science is conducted by humans, which means it's subject to all the same cognitive biases, social pressures, and spectacular failures of judgment that plague every other human endeavor.

The difference is that when scientists get things wrong, the consequences can be particularly dramatic. A poet who writes bad verse hurts nobody but literary critics. A scientist who tests the wrong hypothesis, misinterprets data, or—worst of all—decides to experiment on themselves can end up poisoning entire populations, creating new diseases, or accidentally proving that humans are capable of even more creative forms of self-destruction than previously imagined.

1. Experiments Gone Wild

The history of scientific experimentation is littered with researchers who asked important questions and then answered them in the most dangerous way possible. The problem isn't that these scientists lacked intelligence or training—quite the opposite. They were brilliant people who understood their fields deeply, which made them confident enough to take risks that any reasonable person would consider insane.

Take the curious case of Jesse William Lazear, a physician studying yellow fever transmission in Cuba in 1900. Lazear was convinced that mosquitoes spread the disease, but convincing his colleagues required proof. Rather than designing a careful controlled experiment, Lazear decided to test his hypothesis by allowing infected mosquitoes to bite him. This was actually a reasonable scientific approach, except for the minor detail that yellow fever has a 50% mortality rate.

Lazear's experiment worked perfectly—he contracted yellow fever and died within a week, proving beyond doubt that mosquitoes could transmit the disease. His death provided crucial evidence that led to effective control measures and saved thousands of lives. From a scientific standpoint, his sacrifice was enormously valuable. From a common sense standpoint, there were probably safer ways to test the mosquito theory.

What makes Lazear's story particularly telling is that he wasn't some reckless adventurer; he was a careful researcher who had considered the risks and decided they were acceptable. His letters home show that he understood he might die, but believed the potential benefits to humanity justified the personal cost. This kind of calculated martyrdom runs through many of science's greatest disasters—people making rational decisions that look completely insane in retrospect.

The Stanford Prison Experiment of 1971 represents a different kind of scientific failure: the experiment that revealed more about its creator than its subjects. Philip Zimbardo set out to study how ordinary people behave when placed in positions of authority over others. He recruited college students to play guards and prisoners in a mock jail, expecting to run the experiment for two weeks.

Instead, the situation spiraled out of control within days. The "guards" began psychologically torturing the "prisoners," who showed signs of severe emotional distress. Rather than stopping the experiment, Zimbardo—who was playing the role of prison superintendent—became so absorbed in his artificial world that he lost track of the ethical problems. The experiment was finally shut down after six days, not by Zimbardo, but by a graduate student who was appalled by what she saw.

For decades, the Stanford Prison Experiment was cited as proof that ordinary people will commit atrocities when placed in institutional roles. Recent analysis has revealed a more disturbing truth: the guards didn't become abusive on their own. Zimbardo actively encouraged harsh treatment and coached the guards on how to psychologically manipulate the prisoners. Rather than studying human nature, he had accidentally created a demonstration of how scientists can manipulate research results to confirm their preconceptions.

The experiment's real lesson isn't about the corrupting nature of power—it's about the corrupting nature of having a predetermined conclusion. Zimbardo was so convinced that his theory was correct that he unconsciously designed the experiment to prove it, then ignored evidence that contradicted his expectations. This is confirmation bias in its purest form: the tendency to seek information that supports existing beliefs while ignoring or dismissing contradictory evidence.

What these experiments reveal is that the scientific method, while powerful, is only as reliable as the humans implementing it. Give researchers a theory they want to prove, and they'll often find ways to prove it, even if it means ignoring their own safety or manipulating their subjects. The most dangerous scientific experiments aren't those that test risky hypotheses—they're those conducted by people who are certain they already know the answer.

2. Doctors Who Tested on Themselves

Medical history is full of physicians who took the phrase "first, do no harm" as a personal challenge. These weren't mad scientists twirling their mustaches in underground laboratories—they were respected members of the medical community who genuinely believed that testing treatments on themselves was the ethical thing to do. Their reasoning was impeccable: if a treatment might be dangerous, surely it's better to risk your own life than someone else's.

This logic produced some of medicine's greatest breakthroughs and most spectacular disasters, sometimes simultaneously. Werner Forssmann, a German physician, wanted to prove that cardiac catheterization was possible—inserting a thin tube directly into the heart to diagnose problems. In 1929, with no approval from his superiors and against explicit orders, Forssmann performed the procedure on himself, guiding the catheter through his own blood vessels while watching its progress on an X-ray screen.

The experiment worked perfectly. Forssmann proved that cardiac catheterization was not only possible but relatively safe, laying the groundwork for modern cardiac medicine. He also got fired from his hospital position, had his medical license temporarily suspended, and spent several anxious hours wondering whether he had accidentally killed himself for science. The technique he pioneered would eventually save millions of lives, but at the time, his colleagues thought he was completely insane.

Barry Marshall took self-experimentation to even greater extremes in his quest to prove that stomach ulcers were caused by bacteria rather than stress or spicy food. The medical establishment in the 1980s was convinced that ulcers were a chronic condition requiring lifelong management. Marshall believed they were a simple infection that could be cured with antibiotics, but getting anyone to take his theory seriously required dramatic proof.

So in 1984, Marshall deliberately infected himself with Helicobacter pylori bacteria by drinking a culture that would make a reasonable person vomit just thinking about it. Within days, he developed severe gastritis—the precursor to ulcers. He then cured himself with antibiotics, proving his theory and revolutionizing ulcer treatment. This work eventually earned him a Nobel

Prize, though at the time his colleagues questioned both his scientific methods and his sanity.

The remarkable thing about Marshall's experiment is how casually he approached it. His lab notes from the day he infected himself read more like a grocery list than a record of groundbreaking medical research. He treated deliberately giving himself a potentially serious disease as just another day at the office, which suggests either extraordinary dedication to science or a complete disconnect from normal self-preservation instincts.

Not all medical self-experimentation ended so well. In the 1960s, numerous researchers tested LSD on themselves, convinced they were exploring new frontiers of consciousness and psychology. What they actually discovered was that hallucinogenic drugs affect judgment in ways that make it impossible to objectively study their effects while under their influence. Several careers were destroyed, research programs were shut down, and the entire field of psychedelic research was set back decades by scientists who couldn't resist becoming their own test subjects.

The pattern in all these cases is the same: brilliant people making terrible risk assessments because they were emotionally invested in their theories. Forssmann, Marshall, and the LSD researchers all believed their work was too important to be slowed down by normal safety procedures. They were probably right about the importance, but completely wrong about the necessity of risking their own lives to prove it.

What self-experimenting doctors reveal about human psychology is our tendency to treat ourselves as expendable when pursuing goals we consider meaningful. It's the same mindset that leads entrepreneurs to sacrifice their health for their startups, artists to starve for their craft, and athletes to compete through injuries that will cause lifelong problems. The ability to ignore short-term self-interest in favor of long-term goals is one of humanity's greatest strengths and most dangerous weaknesses.

3. When Faith Collided with Science — and Lost

Nothing brings out humanity's capacity for spectacular wrongness quite like the collision between religious authority and scientific evidence. These conflicts usually follow a predictable pattern: scientists observe something that contradicts established doctrine, religious authorities insist that observation must be wrong, and everyone digs in their heels until the evidence becomes so overwhelming that denial is no longer sustainable.

The Galileo affair is the classic example, though the popular version of the story misses most of what makes it interesting. Galileo wasn't persecuted for doing astronomy—the Catholic Church had been funding astronomical research for centuries and was genuinely interested in improving the calendar. His problems began when he insisted on interpreting his observations in ways that went beyond what his evidence could actually support.

Galileo's telescopic observations clearly showed that Venus had phases, which was impossible under the geocentric model of the universe. This was solid evidence that Venus orbited the sun, not the Earth. But rather than presenting this finding diplomatically, Galileo published a book that mocked anyone who still believed in geocentrism, including his former friend Pope Urban VIII, whom he portrayed as a simpleton in dialogue form.

The Church's response was predictably defensive, but what's often overlooked is that Galileo's science wasn't actually complete enough to definitively prove heliocentrism. His observations were consistent with the sun-centered model, but they were also consistent with Tycho Brahe's hybrid system, in which the planets orbited the sun while the sun orbited the Earth. Galileo rejected this compromise not because his evidence ruled it out, but because he found it intellectually unsatisfying.

The trial that followed was less about science versus religion than about politics, personality, and the dangers of being right in an obnoxious way. Galileo had better evidence than his opponents, but he presented it so condescendingly that he turned potential allies into enemies. His house arrest wasn't punishment for doing science—it was punishment for being an arrogant pain in the ass who happened to also be mostly correct.

The Scopes "Monkey Trial" of 1925 followed a similar pattern, though with roles somewhat reversed. John Scopes was prosecuted for teaching evolution in Tennessee, but the trial quickly became a media circus that had more to do with cultural politics than scientific accuracy. William Jennings Bryan, representing the anti-evolution side, wasn't opposed to all science—he was opposed to the social implications he thought evolution would have.

Bryan's real fear was that teaching evolution would undermine moral behavior by convincing people they were "just animals" with no special responsibilities to God or society. This wasn't an unreasonable concern given how evolutionary theory was being misused to justify racism, eugenics, and social Darwinism. Bryan's mistake was assuming that banning the teaching of evolution would prevent these abuses, rather than addressing the misuse of scientific concepts directly.

The prosecutor Clarence Darrow brilliantly exposed the weakness of Bryan's position by getting him to admit that he didn't interpret all Biblical passages literally—that some were metaphorical or poetic. Once Bryan acknowledged that religious texts required interpretation, his absolute opposition to evolution became harder to defend. But Darrow's victory was largely rhetorical; it didn't actually resolve the underlying tension between scientific and religious worldviews.

What both cases reveal is how cognitive bias affects everyone, including people who should know better. Religious authorities suffered from confirmation bias, interpreting evidence in ways that supported existing beliefs. But scientists weren't immune either—Galileo's certainty about heliocentrism went beyond what his data actually proved, and early evolutionary theorists often let their social prejudices influence their scientific conclusions.

The real tragedy in these science-faith conflicts isn't that religious people opposed scientific findings—it's that both sides often argued past each other instead of engaging with the actual points of disagreement. Most religious objections to science aren't really about empirical facts; they're about meaning, purpose, and moral implications. Most scientific theories don't actually address those concerns, but scientists often present them as if they do, creating unnecessary conflicts.

4. Accidental Discoveries That Were Almost Disasters

Some of science's greatest breakthroughs came from researchers who were trying to do something completely different and stumbled across unexpected results. This sounds romantic and serendipitous until you realize that most accidental discoveries in science are actually evidence of experiments gone wrong. For every penicillin or Post-it note, there are dozens of laboratory accidents that nearly poisoned their discoverers or burned down entire research facilities.

Alexander Fleming's discovery of penicillin is the classic example of beneficial accident, though the full story is considerably messier than the sanitized version taught in schools. Fleming wasn't conducting a careful study of antibacterial agents—he was a notoriously sloppy researcher whose laboratory was legendary for its disorganization. In 1928, he left some bacterial culture plates sitting around his lab while he went on vacation, and when he returned, one plate had been contaminated by a mold that had killed the bacteria around it.

Most researchers would have discarded the contaminated plate and started over, but Fleming was curious enough to investigate further. He identified the mold as Penicillium notatum and confirmed that it produced a substance lethal to many types of bacteria. However, Fleming couldn't figure out how to isolate and purify this substance in useful quantities, so he published a brief paper about his findings and moved on to other projects.

It took another twelve years before Howard Florey and Ernst Boris Chain developed methods for mass-producing penicillin, and even then, the process was so difficult that early production facilities regularly exploded. The mold required very specific growing conditions, the extraction process involved dangerous solvents, and nobody was quite sure why the whole thing worked. Fleming's accidental discovery had to be rediscovered and re-engineered multiple times before it became the life-saving antibiotic we know today.

What makes Fleming's story even more remarkable is how close it came to never happening at all. The contamination occurred because Fleming's laboratory was directly below the mycology lab, where researchers were studying various molds and fungi. Spores from their experiments drifted down through gaps in the floor and contaminated Fleming's bacterial cultures. If the building had been constructed differently, or if Fleming had been tidier, one of medicine's most important discoveries might never have occurred.

The discovery of X-rays followed a similar pattern of controlled accident. Wilhelm Röntgen was experimenting with cathode ray tubes in 1895 when he noticed that a fluorescent screen across his laboratory was glowing, even though the tube was completely covered and shouldn't have been emitting any visible light. Rather than ignoring this anomaly, Röntgen spent weeks investigating, eventually discovering that the tubes were producing invisible radiation that could penetrate most materials.

Röntgen's systematic investigation of this accidental discovery was a masterpiece of careful experimentation. He tested the penetrating power of the rays on different materials, discovered that they could create shadow images of bones inside living tissue, and published his findings with careful documentation and photographic evidence. Within months, doctors around the world were using X-rays for medical diagnosis, revolutionizing healthcare.

But Röntgen's discovery also illustrates the dangers of accidental scientific breakthroughs. Nobody understood that X-rays were harmful to living tissue, so early practitioners exposed themselves and their patients to massive doses of radiation. Many pioneers of radiology developed radiation sickness, lost fingers to radiation burns, or died of cancers caused by their experiments. Thomas Edison's assistant Clarence Dally became one of the first radiation fatalities in America after repeatedly testing X-ray equipment on his own hands.

The pattern in these accidental discoveries is instructive: the accident itself is usually just the beginning. Fleming's moldy plate was useless until other scientists figured out how to turn it into medicine. Röntgen's glowing screen was meaningless until he investigated what was causing it. The real breakthrough comes not from the accident, but from the decision to pay attention to unexpected results rather than dismissing them as experimental errors.

This creates an interesting paradox in scientific research. The most important discoveries often come from experiments that didn't work as intended, but only if the researcher is prepared to recognize that the failure might be more interesting than the original plan. It requires a particular kind of intellectual flexibility—the ability to abandon your hypothesis when the evidence points in a different direction, even if that direction initially seems less important or interesting.

5. Scientific Fails That Now Make Us Laugh

Looking back at the history of science is like reading a collection of confidently wrong predictions and theories that seemed perfectly reasonable at the time. Every generation of scientists has believed they were on the verge of understanding everything, and every generation has been spectacularly wrong about something fundamental. The theories that now seem obviously ridiculous were once defended by brilliant people with impressive credentials and impeccable logic.

Phrenology, the idea that personality could be determined by feeling the bumps on someone's head, dominated psychology for much of the 19th century. Franz Joseph Gall, who developed the theory, wasn't some quack operating out of a carnival tent—he was a respected physician and anatomist who made genuine contributions to understanding brain structure. His basic insight that different brain regions control different functions was actually correct.

Where Gall went wrong was in assuming that these brain regions could be mapped by examining skull shape, and that personality traits were controlled by specific brain bumps that could be felt through the scalp. He divided the human skull into 27 regions, each supposedly corresponding to a different aspect of personality: combativeness, amativeness, philoprogenitiveness (love of offspring), and other traits that sound like they were named by a committee of Victorian academics who had never met actual humans.

Phrenological analysis became incredibly popular because it offered simple, definitive answers to complex psychological questions. Want to know if someone is trustworthy? Check their skull for signs of moral development. Wondering about a potential employee's intelligence? Measure their forehead bumps. The system was completely wrong, but it was wrong in a systematic, scientific-sounding way that satisfied people's desire for certainty about human nature.

What makes phrenology particularly embarrassing in retrospect is how confidently its practitioners made predictions about people's character based on skull measurements. Phrenological societies published detailed charts showing the exact location of various personality traits, and professional phrenologists offered services ranging from career counseling to marriage compatibility assessments. The whole enterprise was built on the assumption that complex human psychology could be reduced to simple physical measurements.

The theory of miasma—the idea that diseases were caused by "bad air"—represents another confident scientific consensus that was almost completely wrong. For centuries, medical authorities believed that cholera, malaria, and other diseases were caused by noxious vapors arising from swamps, garbage, and other sources of unpleasant odors. This theory wasn't entirely unreasonable; many disease outbreaks did seem to correlate with unsanitary conditions and bad smells.

Miasma theory led to some genuinely beneficial public health measures, including improved sanitation and the draining of swamps near cities. These interventions actually did reduce disease transmission, but for reasons that had nothing to do with bad air. Better sanitation reduced waterborne diseases like cholera, and draining swamps eliminated breeding grounds for disease-carrying mosquitoes. The theory was wrong, but the practical applications accidentally addressed the real causes of disease transmission.

The persistence of miasma theory, even after germ theory began providing better explanations for disease transmission, illustrates how difficult it is to abandon established scientific paradigms. Medical authorities had invested decades in miasma-based approaches, built careers on expertise in identifying disease-causing vapors, and developed institutional structures around controlling bad air. Admitting that diseases were actually caused by invisible microorganisms required acknowledging that much of their previous work had been based on fundamentally flawed assumptions.

Perhaps the most embarrassing scientific failure was the confident declaration by Lord Kelvin in 1900 that "there is nothing new to be discovered in physics now." Kelvin, one of the most respected scientists of his era, believed that physics was essentially complete, with only a few minor details left to work out. Within five years, Einstein had published his special theory of relativity, and within a decade, quantum mechanics had revealed that the fundamental nature of reality was far stranger than anyone had imagined.

Kelvin's mistake wasn't stupidity—it was the natural human tendency to assume that current knowledge represents most of what there is to know. Every generation faces the same cognitive bias: we can easily imagine incremental improvements to existing theories, but we struggle to conceive of completely different ways of understanding the world. The possibility that our entire framework might be wrong feels so threatening that we unconsciously dismiss it.

What these scientific failures teach us isn't that scientists are particularly prone to error—it's that confident certainty is often a warning sign rather than a mark of credibility. The researchers who made the biggest breakthroughs were often those who questioned established wisdom rather than defending it. The theories that now seem obviously wrong were once defended by people who couldn't imagine being mistaken about something so fundamental to their worldview.

Chapter 3: Government Blunders

Government is perhaps humanity's most ambitious attempt to organize stupidity at scale. The basic concept is simple enough: get a bunch of people together, agree on some rules, and coordinate activities for mutual benefit. In practice, however, government turns out to be a system for amplifying individual human weaknesses through bureaucratic processes that would make Kafka weep with laughter.

The remarkable thing about government failures isn't their frequency—any system involving humans will fail regularly—but their spectacular creativity. Private sector mistakes are usually variations on familiar themes: bad products, poor service, financial mismanagement. Government mistakes, by contrast, can achieve levels of absurdity that would seem implausible in fiction. When bureaucrats set their minds to solving a problem, they can create new categories of disaster that nobody had previously imagined possible.

1. The Most Expensive Bureaucratic Mistakes Ever Made

When governments make mistakes, they don't just waste a little money or cause minor inconvenience—they invent entirely new ways to squander resources on a scale that would impress ancient pharaohs. The key ingredient is always the same: take a simple problem, create a complex bureaucratic solution, then be genuinely surprised when that solution generates ten new problems, each more expensive than the original.

The Healthcare.gov rollout in 2013 is a perfect example of how government procurement can turn a straightforward task into a multibillion-dollar catastrophe. The assignment was conceptually simple: build a website where people could shop for health insurance. The private sector builds e-commerce sites every day, many handling far more complex transactions with millions of users. But when the federal government tackled this problem, they managed to create a system that crashed under normal usage, lost user data, and cost more than developing Instagram, Twitter, and Snapchat combined.

The root cause wasn't technical incompetence—though there was plenty of that—but the bureaucratic process used to design and build the system. Instead of hiring one company to build a cohesive website, the government divided the project among dozens of contractors, each responsible for different components. Nobody was in charge of making sure these components would work together, and the testing process was so fragmented that major integration problems weren't discovered until launch day.

What made the disaster even more expensive was the government's response to the initial failure. Rather than stepping back and redesigning the procurement process, officials doubled down, hiring additional contractors to fix the problems created by the original contractors. The result was a digital equivalent of too many cooks in the kitchen, with dozens of companies simultaneously modifying code, often overwriting each other's work. The final cost exceeded $2 billion, roughly equivalent to buying a small country.

The Berlin Brandenburg Airport represents an even more spectacular example of how bureaucratic processes can transform routine projects into financial disasters. The airport was supposed to be a straightforward infrastructure project: build a modern airport to replace Berlin's aging facilities. Ground was broken in 2006 with a planned opening date of 2011 and a budget of €2.83 billion. The airport finally opened in 2020 with a total cost exceeding €7 billion—nearly triple the original budget.

The delays weren't caused by technical challenges that would stump normal engineers, but by an approval process so complex that no human could navigate it successfully. The fire safety system alone required approval from 17 different agencies, each with contradictory requirements. When engineers designed a system that satisfied Agency A's requirements, it would violate Agency B's standards. Modifying the design to satisfy Agency B would then create problems with Agency C, and so forth.

The approval process became a bureaucratic version of whack-a-mole, with each solution creating new problems that required additional approvals from additional agencies. Meanwhile, the partially completed airport sat empty for nearly a decade, accumulating maintenance costs and becoming increasingly obsolete as aviation technology advanced. By the time it opened, some of its systems were already due for replacement.

What these failures reveal is the fundamental mismatch between how bureaucracies work and how complex projects actually get completed. Bureaucratic processes are designed to minimize individual responsibility by distributing decision-making across multiple agencies and approval layers. This works fine for routine tasks with clear precedents, but it breaks down completely when applied to novel challenges that require coordination and adaptability.

The real cost of bureaucratic mistakes isn't just the wasted money—it's the opportunity cost of projects that never get attempted because everyone assumes they'll turn into expensive disasters. When building a website costs

$2 billion and opening an airport takes 14 years, rational policymakers become reluctant to tackle genuinely difficult challenges like infrastructure modernization or healthcare system reform.

2. When Paperwork Killed Innovation

The relationship between bureaucratic procedure and human innovation is roughly equivalent to the relationship between concrete boots and Olympic swimming. Bureaucracies exist to ensure consistency, prevent errors, and distribute responsibility across multiple decision-makers. Innovation requires speed, risk-taking, and the ability to make decisions without knowing all the answers. Asking a bureaucracy to foster innovation is like asking a submarine to fly—technically possible, but likely to end badly for everyone involved.

The U.S. Patent Office provides a fascinating case study in how bureaucratic processes can inadvertently stifle the very innovation they're designed to protect. In 1899, Charles H. Duell, the Commissioner of Patents, allegedly declared that "everything that can be invented has been invented" and suggested that the patent office should be closed. While this specific quote is probably apocryphal, it captures the mindset that led to decades of patent applications being rejected for innovations that were "obviously impossible".

The pattern was always the same: inventors would submit applications for devices that violated the conventional wisdom of their era, patent examiners would reject them without serious consideration, and years later the same innovations would revolutionize entire industries. The Wright brothers' patent application for their flying machine was initially rejected because heavier-than-air flight was considered impossible. Lee de Forest's patent for the vacuum tube was approved only after he demonstrated a working prototype, because the patent examiner couldn't understand how it was supposed to function.

What made these rejections particularly frustrating was that they weren't based on technical analysis, but on bureaucratic risk aversion. Patent examiners were punished for approving applications that later proved invalid, but rarely criticized for rejecting applications that later proved valuable. This created an institutional bias toward saying "no" to anything that seemed unusual or unprecedented. The system was perfectly designed to protect the patent office from embarrassment, and completely unsuited to encouraging innovative thinking.

The Soviet Union's approach to innovation provides an even more dramatic example of how bureaucratic control can suppress technological progress. The centrally planned economy required all research and development to be approved through a complex hierarchy of committees, each responsible for ensuring that proposed innovations aligned with official priorities and didn't threaten existing production targets.

This system worked reasonably well for incremental improvements to existing technologies—making steel production slightly more efficient, improving agricultural yields, optimizing manufacturing processes. But it was devastating for breakthrough innovations that couldn't be easily categorized or that might disrupt existing economic plans. Computer technology, for example, was delayed for decades because planners couldn't figure out how to integrate it into five-year production goals.

The most tragic example was the fate of Soviet cybernetics research in the 1950s and 1960s. Soviet scientists were among the world's leaders in early computer science and information theory, but their research was repeatedly suppressed because it didn't fit into Marxist economic theory. The idea that information could be treated as a commodity, or that decentralized decision-making might be more efficient than central planning, was ideologically unacceptable regardless of the scientific evidence.

By the time Soviet leadership recognized the importance of computer technology, they were decades behind the West and had lost most of their early advantages in the field. The bureaucratic system designed to ensure ideological purity had inadvertently crippled the Soviet Union's ability to compete in the most important technological revolution of the 20th century.

The lesson from these cases isn't that bureaucracy is inherently evil—it's that bureaucratic processes optimized for one set of goals (consistency, risk management, ideological compliance) can be completely unsuited for achieving other goals (innovation, adaptability, technological progress). When institutions lose sight of their ultimate purpose and focus instead on following procedures, they can end up systematically undermining their own mission.

3. Wars Started by Translation Errors

Language barriers have been causing problems since humans first developed different ways of saying "hello," but when governments get involved, simple miscommunications can escalate into international conflicts that leave historians scratching their heads and wondering how anyone could be that stupid. The problem isn't usually the translators themselves—it's the politicians who receive translated messages and somehow conclude that the only reasonable response involves mobilizing armies.

The Pig War of 1859 between the United States and Britain is the classic example of diplomatic translation going catastrophically wrong. The crisis began when an American farmer shot a British pig, but it escalated because of a series of mistranslations and misunderstandings between local officials who spoke different varieties of English but assumed they understood each other perfectly.

The British colonial governor interpreted American complaints about "trespassing livestock" as a broader challenge to British sovereignty over San Juan Island. The American territorial governor read British objections to "unauthorized settlement" as a threat to evict all American residents. Neither side was actually talking about the same issues, but both were confident they understood what the other side meant. Within weeks, hundreds of troops were facing each other across disputed potato gardens, all because nobody had bothered to clarify what they were actually arguing about.

What made the situation even more absurd was that both governments eventually realized the dispute was ridiculous, but couldn't figure out how to back down without losing face. The British couldn't withdraw their forces because that would suggest they were afraid of American farmers. The Americans couldn't withdraw because that would imply they were abandoning their citizens to foreign oppression. The standoff continued for months, with both sides looking for a dignified way to end a conflict that nobody wanted to be fighting.

The Ems Telegram incident of 1870 shows how deliberate mistranslation can be used to manufacture pretexts for wars that politicians want to fight anyway. Otto von Bismarck, the Prussian chancellor, received a diplomatic telegram describing a minor protocol dispute between the Prussian king and the French ambassador. Rather than forwarding the message accurately, Bismarck edited it to make both sides sound more insulting and confrontational.

Bismarck's edited version transformed a routine diplomatic exchange into an apparent series of mutual insults. When published in newspapers, it created exactly the public outrage Bismarck needed to justify the Franco-Prussian War he had been planning. The French government, seeing the edited telegram, concluded that Prussia was deliberately humiliating France and declared war within days. Neither the Prussian king nor the French ambassador had actually said anything particularly offensive, but their words had been weaponized through selective mistranslation.

The remarkable thing about the Ems Telegram is how little effort Bismarck put into making his edits believable. Contemporary observers could see that the published version didn't match the original diplomatic language, but public opinion had already been inflamed beyond the point where accuracy mattered. Sometimes mistranslation works not because it's convincing, but because it tells people what they already want to believe.

More recently, translation errors have continued to complicate international relations in ways that would be hilarious if they weren't so potentially dangerous. During the Cold War, Soviet Premier Nikita Khrushchev's famous declaration "We will bury you" was initially translated as a military threat, contributing to American fears about Soviet aggression. The phrase actually meant "We will outlast you" or "We will be present at your funeral"—a prediction about economic competition rather than a threat of nuclear war.

The mistranslation shaped American foreign policy for years, contributing to military buildups and diplomatic tensions that might have been avoided with more careful interpretation. By the time the error was recognized and corrected, the political damage had already been done. Both sides had made decisions based on the misunderstanding, creating a spiral of mistrust that took decades to resolve.

What these translation disasters reveal is how much international relations depend on the assumption that everyone means what they appear to be saying. When that assumption breaks down—whether through honest error, cultural misunderstanding, or deliberate manipulation—the results can be far more serious than simple communication problems between individuals. At the international level, mistranslation doesn't just cause confusion; it can reshape the geopolitical landscape for generations.

4. Governments That Outlawed Common Sense

Throughout history, legislators have demonstrated a remarkable talent for creating laws that solve non-existent problems, regulate impossible behaviors, and generally make normal human activities unnecessarily complicated. The most impressive examples don't just ban specific actions—they outlaw entire categories of common sense, creating legal frameworks so absurd that compliance would require abandoning basic logic.

The prohibition of alcohol in the United States from 1920 to 1933 represents perhaps the most spectacular example of government attempting to legislate human nature out of existence. The 18th Amendment and the

Volstead Act didn't just ban alcohol consumption—they created a legal structure that made virtually every adult

American in the country a potential criminal. The law didn't just prohibit selling alcohol—it banned manufacturing, transporting, importing, or even possessing alcoholic beverages. This meant that having a bottle of wine in your cellar, serving beer at a private party, or taking communion with real wine all became federal crimes punishable by imprisonment.

The Volstead Act created a legal framework so comprehensive in its absurdity that enforcement was literally impossible. Prohibition agents were expected to monitor every basement, barn, and bathtub in America to ensure nobody was fermenting grape juice or distilling grain alcohol. The law turned millions of law-abiding citizens into criminals overnight, created a massive black market controlled by organized crime, and generated corruption on a scale that would make a banana republic blush.

What makes Prohibition particularly instructive is how it demonstrates the government's capacity to ignore obvious cause-and-effect relationships when ideology is involved. Within months of the law taking effect, alcohol consumption actually increased in many areas, crime rates skyrocketed, and government revenues plummeted due to lost tax revenue. Rather than acknowledging these problems, officials responded by making enforcement even more aggressive, as if the solution to a failed policy was simply more failure.

The Soviet Union's approach to agriculture under Stalin provides an even more dramatic example of government attempting to outlaw economic reality through legislative fiat. The doctrine of Lysenkoism, promoted by biologist Trofim Lysenko, rejected established genetics in favor of theories that aligned better with Marxist ideology. According to Lysenko, plants could be trained to behave in ways that supported socialist agricultural goals, regardless of their biological limitations.

Lysenko convinced Stalin that wheat could be taught to grow in climates where it had never survived, that crop yields could be doubled through ideological education of farmers, and that Darwin's theory of evolution was a capitalist plot to justify inequality. These ideas were not only scientifically nonsensical but directly contradicted the practical experience of every farmer in the Soviet Union. Nevertheless, they became official policy, enforced through arrests and executions of scientists who questioned them.

The result was a series of famines that killed millions of people, not because of drought or natural disasters, but because the government had literally outlawed effective farming techniques. Farmers who used traditional methods that actually worked were arrested for "sabotage," while those who followed Lysenko's scientifically impossible recommendations watched their crops fail year after year. The policy continued for decades, devastating Soviet agriculture and contributing to chronic food shortages that persisted until the collapse of the communist system.

What both Prohibition and Lysenkoism reveal is the danger of laws that attempt to regulate fundamental aspects of human nature or natural processes. When governments decide that reality is inconvenient and try to legislate it out of existence, they don't change reality—they just create massive incentives for people to ignore or circumvent the law. The more comprehensive the prohibition, the more creative people become in finding ways around it.

5. Political Gaffes That Changed History

Politicians have been saying stupid things in public for as long as there have been politicians and audiences to hear them. Most political gaffes are quickly forgotten, remembered only by opposition researchers and late-night comedians. But occasionally, a politician manages to say something so spectacularly wrong-headed, at such a perfectly wrong moment, that it reshapes the entire political landscape. These aren't simple slips of the tongue—they're verbal nuclear explosions that reveal fundamental misunderstandings about reality.

"Let them eat cake" is probably history's most famous political gaffe, even though Marie Antoinette never actually said it. The phrase was attributed to her by revolutionaries who wanted to illustrate the French aristocracy's complete disconnection from the suffering of ordinary people. Whether she said it or not, the sentiment perfectly captured why the French Revolution was inevitable: the ruling class had become so isolated from reality that they couldn't understand why starving peasants were upset about bread shortages.

The real tragedy of the "let them eat cake" story isn't that Marie Antoinette was cruel or callous—contemporary accounts suggest she was actually more sympathetic to common people than most aristocrats of her era. The tragedy is that the French government had become so dysfunctional that reasonable policy discussions were impossible. By the time revolution broke out, positions had become so polarized that any attempt at compromise was seen as betrayal by both sides.

More recently, President Gerald Ford's declaration during a 1976 debate that "there is no Soviet domination of Eastern Europe" managed to undermine his entire foreign policy credibility in a single sentence. Ford's statement was technically true in the narrow sense that Eastern European countries maintained their own governments and legal systems, but it completely ignored the reality that those governments were Soviet puppets with no real independence.

What made Ford's gaffe particularly damaging was its timing. The debate occurred at the height of the Cold War, when American voters were deeply concerned about Soviet expansionism. Ford's apparent lack of awareness about basic geopolitical realities suggested that he wasn't competent to manage America's foreign policy during a dangerous period. The comment is widely credited with costing him the 1976 election.

The remarkable thing about Ford's mistake is that he actually understood the situation in Eastern Europe perfectly well—he had been dealing with Soviet-controlled governments for years as president. His error was linguistic rather than substantive: he used precise diplomatic language in a context that called for plain speaking. The lesson is that political communication isn't just about accuracy; it's about conveying understanding in ways that audiences can relate to.

Perhaps the most consequential political gaffe in recent history was British Prime Minister Neville Chamberlain's declaration of "peace for our time" after signing the Munich Agreement with Hitler in 1938. Chamberlain genuinely believed that appeasing German territorial demands would prevent a larger war, and his approach had strong support from both the British public and Parliament. The problem was that his assessment of Hitler's intentions was completely wrong.

Chamberlain's error wasn't stupidity or cowardice—it was a fundamental misunderstanding of what kind of person he was dealing with. He approached Hitler as if he were a conventional European leader who could be satisfied through negotiation and compromise. Hitler, however, was never going to be satisfied with partial victories when total domination seemed achievable. Chamberlain's diplomatic framework was perfectly suited for dealing with rational actors, but completely inadequate for handling a megalomaniacal dictator.

The "peace for our time" declaration became a symbol of the dangers of appeasement, but the real lesson is more subtle. Chamberlain's mistake wasn't that he preferred negotiation to war—reasonable people will always prefer peaceful solutions when they're available. His mistake was assuming that his preferred solution was actually possible without accurately assessing whether the other party shared his commitment to peaceful resolution.

What all these gaffes reveal is how political communication can take on a life of its own, independent of the speaker's actual beliefs or intentions. Politicians often become prisoners of their own rhetoric, forced to defend positions that made sense in one context but become indefensible when circumstances change. The most dangerous political gaffes aren't those that reveal stupidity, but those that reveal how disconnected leaders can become from the reality their policies are supposed to address.

Chapter 4: Inventors Who Regretted Their Inventions

The relationship between scientific progress and human wisdom has always been complicated, but nowhere is this more evident than in the stories of inventors who created something revolutionary and then spent the rest of their lives wishing they hadn't. These aren't mad scientists cackling over doomsday devices—they're thoughtful people who solved important problems and then watched in horror as humanity found the most destructive possible applications for their solutions.

The pattern is always the same: identify a genuine need, develop an elegant solution, celebrate the breakthrough, then gradually realize that you've handed the human race a new and improved method of making life worse for everyone. The most tragic cases are those where the inventor lived long enough to see their creation's full impact on the world, spending their final years as reluctant witnesses to the unintended consequences of their genius.

1. Creators Who Hated Their Own Creations

Robert Oppenheimer's transformation from celebrated physicist to tormented prophet of doom represents the classic arc of inventive regret. The Manhattan Project brought together the finest scientific minds of the era to solve what seemed like a straightforward engineering problem: how to release the energy stored in atomic nuclei. The physics was fascinating, the mathematics was elegant, and the sense of patriotic mission was overwhelming. Nobody involved expected to create a weapon that would fundamentally change the nature of human conflict.

Oppenheimer's famous reaction to the Trinity test—"Now I am become Death, destroyer of worlds"—wasn't dramatic posturing for the cameras. It was the moment when a brilliant physicist realized that he had helped create something that could end human civilization. The scientific problem they had been asked to solve was real: how to end World War II as quickly as possible with minimal Allied casualties. The solution they developed was technically perfect and strategically effective. It was also morally catastrophic.

What makes Oppenheimer's regret particularly poignant is that he never questioned the original decision to build the bomb. Even in his darkest moments, he acknowledged that stopping Nazi Germany from developing nuclear weapons first was essential. His torment came from watching how nuclear weapons changed international relations, creating a balance of terror that made every future conflict potentially apocalyptic. He had solved the immediate problem of ending World War II, but created the much larger problem of preventing World War III.

Mikhail Kalashnikov experienced a similar trajectory with his invention of the AK-47 assault rifle. Kalashnikov was a tank mechanic in the Soviet Army when he was wounded during the Battle of Bryansk in 1941. While recovering in the hospital, he became obsessed with designing a reliable automatic weapon that would give Soviet forces an advantage against German troops who were better equipped with submachine guns.

Kalashnikov's design brilliance lay in creating a weapon that was both highly effective and virtually indestructible. The AK-47 could function in mud, sand, water, and extreme temperatures without jamming or misfiring. It was so simple that child soldiers could operate and maintain it with minimal training. These features made it perfect for the Soviet military's needs, but they also made it the weapon of choice for guerrilla fighters, terrorists, and criminal organizations worldwide.

By the end of his life, Kalashnikov estimated that his design had been used to kill more people than any other individual weapon in history. Unlike Oppenheimer, who always understood the destructive potential of nuclear weapons, Kalashnikov genuinely believed he was creating a tool for national defense. He never anticipated that his rifle would become the preferred instrument of violence for every rebel group, drug cartel, and extremist organization on the planet.

Kalashnikov's final interviews reveal a man struggling to reconcile his patriotic intentions with the global consequences of his invention. He remained proud of the technical achievement—the AK-47 is genuinely one of the finest pieces of military engineering ever created. But he was deeply troubled by its proliferation and misuse, particularly its role in conflicts that had nothing to do with defending the Soviet Union.

Both Oppenheimer and Kalashnikov faced the same fundamental problem: they were asked to solve technical challenges without being given any way to control how their solutions would be used. They created tools that worked exactly as designed, but in contexts far removed from the original problem they were meant to address. This highlights one of the central dilemmas of technological progress—the gap between what we can create and what we should create.

2. Good Ideas Gone Catastrophic

Thomas Midgley Jr. has the dubious distinction of being responsible for more environmental damage than any other individual in human history, despite having the best of intentions throughout his career. Midgley wasn't an evil genius plotting to destroy the planet—he was a brilliant chemist who solved two major problems of his era with innovations that seemed not only harmless but beneficial at the time.

In the 1920s, automobile engines suffered from a problem called "knocking"—irregular combustion that reduced performance and could damage the engine. Midgley discovered that adding tetraethyl lead to gasoline eliminated this problem completely, making cars more efficient and reliable. The solution was so elegant that leaded gasoline became the industry standard worldwide, remaining in use for decades.

Around the same time, Midgley tackled another pressing problem: refrigerators that used toxic gases like ammonia and sulfur dioxide as coolants. These early refrigerators occasionally leaked, killing entire families in their sleep. Midgley developed chlorofluorocarbons (CFCs) as a safer alternative—chemicals that were non-toxic, non-flammable, and worked perfectly in refrigeration systems. To demonstrate their safety, he once inhaled CFC vapor at a scientific conference and then exhaled it to blow out a candle.

Both innovations were hailed as major advances in public safety and convenience. Leaded gasoline improved automotive performance while reducing maintenance costs. CFCs made refrigeration safe for home use, revolutionizing food preservation and public health. Midgley received awards from scientific societies, became wealthy from his patents, and was celebrated as one of America's most important inventors.

The environmental consequences of both inventions only became apparent decades later. Lead from gasoline created a global epidemic of lead poisoning, causing learning disabilities, behavioral problems, and reduced intelligence in entire generations of children. CFCs, released into the atmosphere, began destroying the ozone layer that protects Earth from harmful ultraviolet radiation.

What makes Midgley's story particularly tragic is that both problems were technically solvable without his "solutions." Alternative anti-knock compounds existed but were more expensive to produce. Mechanical refrigeration systems could have been made safer through better engineering and safety standards. Midgley's innovations were chosen not because they were the only options available, but because they were the most profitable and convenient.

The irony reached its peak when Midgley, paralyzed by polio in his later years, invented an elaborate system of pulleys and ropes to help transfer himself from bed to wheelchair. True to form, this final invention also turned against him—he became entangled in the contraption and strangled to death in 1944. Even his attempts to solve personal problems created new dangers.

Midgley's career illustrates the fundamental problem with technological solutions that seem too good to be true: they usually are. His inventions solved immediate, visible problems (engine knock, refrigerator toxicity) while creating delayed, invisible problems (atmospheric pollution, ozone depletion). This temporal mismatch between benefits and costs makes it almost impossible to make fully informed decisions about new technologies.

3. Discoveries That Led to Tragedy

The story of Fritz Haber represents one of science's most morally complex figures—a man who made discoveries that both saved millions of lives and enabled some of history's worst atrocities. Haber developed the process for synthesizing ammonia from nitrogen and hydrogen, a breakthrough that revolutionized agriculture by making cheap fertilizer possible. His work is estimated to have enabled the population growth that feeds about half the world's current population.

The same chemical knowledge that made Haber a hero of agriculture also made him the father of chemical warfare. During World War I, he personally supervised the first use of chlorine gas against Allied forces at the Second Battle of Ypres in 1915. Haber believed that chemical weapons would make wars shorter and less deadly by forcing quick decisions rather than prolonged battles. Instead, they added a new dimension of horror to an already brutal conflict.

Haber's wife Clara, also a chemist, was so horrified by her husband's work on poison gas that she shot herself with his service pistol. Her suicide note reportedly read, "It is a perversion of the ideals of science to use it as means of destruction." Haber, meanwhile, continued his chemical weapons research, convinced that he was serving his country and advancing the cause of science.

The tragedy deepened when Haber's research on pesticides was later adapted by the Nazi regime to create Zyklon B, the gas used in concentration camps during the Holocaust. Haber himself, despite his service to Germany during World War I, was forced to flee the country in 1933 because of his Jewish heritage. He died in exile, never knowing that his chemical innovations would be used to murder millions of people, including members of his own extended family.

Haber's story illustrates the impossible position of scientists working on dual-use technologies—research that has both beneficial and harmful applications. His ammonia synthesis process genuinely solved the problem of global food security, enabling population growth that would have been impossible otherwise. But the same chemical knowledge made industrial-scale murder possible in ways that previous generations could never have imagined.

Nobel's invention of dynamite follows a similar pattern of beneficial innovation with catastrophic applications. Alfred Nobel developed dynamite to make mining and construction safer—early explosives were so unstable that they frequently killed the workers trying to use them. Dynamite was stable, predictable, and far safer to handle than previous explosives. It revolutionized construction, enabling projects like the Panama Canal and the transcontinental railroads.

But dynamite also transformed warfare, making it possible to cause destruction on a scale previously unimaginable. Nobel was horrified when a French newspaper mistakenly published his obituary in 1888, calling him the "merchant of death" who had made his fortune by finding new ways to kill people. The obituary reportedly read, "Dr. Alfred Nobel, who became rich by finding ways to kill more people faster than ever before, died yesterday".

This premature obituary motivated Nobel to establish the Nobel Prizes, hoping to be remembered for promoting peace and human achievement rather than destruction. But the weapons made possible by his innovations continued to evolve, eventually leading to the high explosives that made nuclear weapons possible. Nobel's attempt to atone for his invention through philanthropy was admirable, but it couldn't undo the military revolution he had initiated.

What both Haber and Nobel discovered is that scientific knowledge, once released into the world, takes on a life of its own. Inventors can control the initial application of their discoveries, but they cannot control how that knowledge will be used by future generations with different priorities and moral frameworks. The same scientific principles that enable beneficial applications will inevitably enable harmful ones as well.

4. Inventions That Caused More Harm Than Help

The development of leaded gasoline represents one of the most clear-cut cases of an invention that caused far more harm than good, yet it remained in widespread use for decades after its dangers became apparent. The story begins with a legitimate problem: early automobile engines suffered from irregular combustion that reduced performance and could damage expensive components. Engineers tried dozens of different additives before discovering that tetraethyl lead eliminated the problem completely.

From a purely technical standpoint, leaded gasoline was a remarkable success. It made cars more reliable, improved fuel efficiency, and reduced maintenance costs. The additive was so effective that it became the global standard for automotive fuel, used in virtually every country for more than fifty years. The petroleum industry promoted it as a major advance in automotive technology, which in purely mechanical terms, it actually was.

The health consequences, however, were catastrophic. Lead is a neurotoxin that accumulates in the body over time, causing permanent damage to the nervous system, particularly in developing children. Decades of leaded gasoline use created a global epidemic of lead poisoning, exposing entire generations to a substance that reduced intelligence, increased aggressive behavior, and caused learning disabilities.

What makes the leaded gasoline story particularly infuriating is that the health risks were known from the beginning. Workers at early tetraethyl lead production facilities frequently suffered from lead poisoning, and several died from acute exposure. These incidents were documented in medical journals and reported in newspapers, but the petroleum industry successfully argued that automotive exposure levels would be much lower than industrial exposure levels.

The argument was technically true but practically irrelevant. While individual exposure from each tank of gasoline was indeed small, the cumulative effect of millions of cars burning leaded fuel created atmospheric lead levels that exceeded industrial safety standards in many urban areas. Children living near highways showed blood lead levels comparable to those of workers in lead mines.

The transition away from leaded gasoline began only in the 1970s, and even then, it was driven more by the needs of catalytic converters than by health concerns. Lead poisoned the catalysts used in emission control systems, making it impossible to meet new air quality standards. The petroleum industry, which had resisted health-based arguments for decades, quickly developed lead-free alternatives when mechanical necessity demanded them.

Asbestos presents an even more tragic example of a beneficial material that turned into a public health catastrophe. For most of the 20th century, asbestos was considered a miracle material—it was fireproof, chemically inert, strong, and relatively inexpensive. It was used in everything from building insulation to brake pads, protecting countless people from fires and mechanical failures.

The fire protection provided by asbestos was real and significant. Buildings constructed with asbestos materials were genuinely safer from fire damage, and asbestos brake linings prevented automotive accidents. During World War II, asbestos insulation in ships and aircraft probably saved thousands of lives by preventing fires that would have been fatal in combat conditions.

But asbestos fibers, when inhaled, cause mesothelioma and other fatal lung diseases. The latency period between exposure and disease onset is typically 20-40 years, which meant that the health consequences didn't become apparent until millions of people had already been exposed. By the time the connection between asbestos and lung disease was established, entire industries had been built around materials that were slowly killing their workers.

What makes the asbestos story particularly tragic is that safer alternatives existed for most applications, but they were more expensive or less convenient. Asbestos was chosen not because it was the only material that could provide fire protection, but because it was the cheapest and most versatile option available. Economic considerations trumped safety concerns, even after the health risks became apparent.

Both leaded gasoline and asbestos illustrate a fundamental problem with evaluating technological benefits and risks. The benefits of new technologies are usually immediate and obvious, while the costs are often delayed and difficult to measure. This creates a systematic bias toward adopting technologies that provide short-term advantages while imposing long-term costs that only become apparent after widespread adoption makes reversal difficult and expensive.

The story of John von Neumann and the development of computer architecture illustrates how brilliant people can create technologies with consequences far beyond anything they originally imagined. Von Neumann was working on mathematical problems related to nuclear weapons design when he realized that electronic computers could revolutionize not just weapons research, but virtually every aspect of human activity that involved information processing.

Von Neumann's contributions to computer science were foundational—the stored-program architecture that bears his name is still the basis for virtually all modern computers. His work made possible everything from scientific research to global communications to the digital revolution that has transformed human society. From a purely technical standpoint, his innovations were unquestionably beneficial to humanity.

But von Neumann also foresaw that computer technology would fundamentally alter the balance of power in human societies, concentrating unprecedented capabilities in the hands of whoever controlled the most advanced systems. He worried that artificial intelligence, which he considered inevitable, might make human decision-making obsolete. In his final years, he expressed concern that technological progress was outpacing human wisdom.

Von Neumann's fears have proven remarkably prescient. Computer technology has indeed concentrated power in ways that would have been impossible in earlier eras, enabling mass surveillance, automated warfare, and economic disruption on a global scale. The same computational power that enables scientific breakthroughs also enables cyber-warfare, financial manipulation, and social media platforms designed to exploit human psychological weaknesses.

What troubled von Neumann most was his recognition that technological development had become autonomous—advancing according to its own logic rather than human intentions. He had helped create tools that were powerful enough to reshape civilization, but there was no mechanism for ensuring they would be used wisely. The genie was out of the bottle, and even its creator couldn't control what it would do next.

The development of the internet follows a similar pattern of beneficial intentions producing unintended consequences. The original ARPANET was designed by researchers who genuinely wanted to improve scientific communication and make computer resources more accessible. The system they created was decentralized, resilient, and designed to promote the free exchange of information.

These features made the internet incredibly valuable for legitimate research and communication, but they also made it perfect for activities that its creators never anticipated: cybercrime, terrorism coordination, and the spread of disinformation. The same decentralized architecture that makes the internet resilient against technical failures also makes it nearly impossible to control or regulate effectively.

The inventors of the World Wide Web, particularly Tim Berners-Lee, have expressed similar concerns about how their creation has evolved. Berners-Lee envisioned a system that would democratize access to information and enable collaboration on a global scale. Instead, the web has become dominated by a few large corporations that use sophisticated algorithms to manipulate user behavior for profit.

What all these cases reveal is the fundamental unpredictability of technological systems once they reach a certain level of complexity. Von Neumann, the ARPANET designers, and the web's creators all understood the immediate applications of their technologies, but they couldn't foresee how those technologies would evolve when deployed at global scale with billions of users pursuing their own objectives.

The lesson isn't that we should stop creating powerful technologies—the benefits are often too significant to ignore. Rather, it's that we need better mechanisms for anticipating and managing the unintended consequences of innovations that can reshape society. The most dangerous technologies aren't necessarily those designed for destructive purposes, but those designed for beneficial purposes that turn out to have emergent properties their creators never imagined.

Chapter 5: Corporate Disasters

The business world operates on the theory that competition and profit motives will drive companies to make rational decisions that benefit both themselves and their customers. In practice, however, corporations are run by humans, which means they're subject to all the same cognitive biases, groupthink, and spectacular failures of judgment that plague every other human institution. The main difference is that when businesses make catastrophically bad decisions, they often do so with remarkable efficiency and impressive scale.

Corporate failures are particularly fascinating because they typically involve intelligent people with access to extensive market research, sophisticated analytical tools, and powerful incentives to get things right. When these advantages combine to produce decisions that seem obviously wrong in retrospect, it usually reveals something important about how human psychology interacts with organizational structures and market pressures.

1. The Worst Marketing Decisions Ever

New Coke represents perhaps the purest example of how market research can lead companies directly into disaster when filtered through corporate groupthink and executive ego. In 1985, Coca-Cola executives were genuinely concerned about losing market share to Pepsi, which had been gaining ground through taste-test marketing campaigns. Their solution was to reformulate their flagship product to taste more like their main competitor, which is roughly equivalent to McDonald's deciding to become more like Burger King by eliminating the Big Mac.

The decision wasn't made carelessly—Coca-Cola conducted extensive market research, including 200,000 taste tests that consistently showed consumers preferred the new formula. The problem was that the research measured taste preferences in isolation, without considering the emotional and cultural significance of the original product. Coca-Cola wasn't just a soft drink; it was a cultural institution with symbolic meaning that couldn't be captured in blind taste tests.

When New Coke launched, the public reaction was immediate and overwhelmingly negative. Consumers didn't just dislike the new formula—they felt betrayed by a company they had trusted for decades. The backlash was so intense that Coca-Cola received over 400,000 complaints in the first few months, and some consumers began hoarding bottles of the original formula as if preparing for the apocalypse.

What makes the New Coke disaster particularly instructive is that Coca-Cola's market research was technically accurate—people did prefer the taste of the new formula when sampled blind. But the research completely missed the most important factor: people's relationship with brands isn't purely rational. They form emotional attachments that can't be measured through conventional market research techniques.

The company was forced to bring back the original formula as "Coca-Cola Classic" within 79 days, in what became one of the most expensive marketing reversals in corporate history. Ironically, the controversy probably helped Coca-Cola in the long run by demonstrating how passionately consumers felt about the brand, but the short-term damage to executive credibility was enormous.

Ford's introduction of the Edsel in 1957 represents a different type of marketing failure—the triumph of internal corporate logic over external market reality. Ford executives convinced themselves that American consumers wanted a medium-priced car that split the difference between economy and luxury vehicles. This conclusion was based on demographic analysis showing a growing middle class with disposable income for automotive upgrades.

The analysis was statistically sound, but it ignored a crucial shift in consumer behavior that was happening simultaneously. Rather than buying more expensive cars in the same traditional categories, consumers were beginning to prioritize style, performance, and brand image over simple price positioning. They wanted cars that made statements about their personalities, not cars that fit into predetermined market segments.

Ford spent three years and $400 million developing the Edsel, conducting market research that consistently confirmed their assumptions about consumer demand for medium-priced vehicles. But by the time the car launched, consumer preferences had shifted toward either economy cars that provided maximum value or distinctive vehicles that expressed individual style. The Edsel, designed to appeal to everyone, ended up appealing to almost no one.

The Edsel's failure wasn't due to poor quality or inappropriate pricing—it was a competently built car that delivered exactly what Ford's research suggested consumers wanted. The problem was that Ford's research was measuring what people said they wanted rather than observing what they actually bought. Consumer preferences had evolved faster than corporate planning cycles, leaving Ford with a solution to a problem that no longer existed.

What both New Coke and the Edsel reveal is how corporate decision-making can become disconnected from market reality when companies rely too heavily on abstract data rather than intuitive understanding of their customers. Both companies had access to sophisticated research capabilities, but they used those capabilities to confirm preexisting assumptions rather than challenge them.

2. The Fall of "Too Big to Fail" Companies

Enron's collapse in 2001 represents one of the most spectacular examples of how corporate arrogance and financial manipulation can destroy even the largest and most successful companies. At its peak, Enron was the seventh-largest corporation in America, celebrated for its innovative business model and aggressive growth strategy. The company's executives were featured on magazine covers as visionary leaders who had revolutionized the energy industry.

The innovation that made Enron famous was treating energy like a financial commodity that could be traded, hedged, and securitized like stocks or bonds. This approach generated enormous profits during the 1990s and created new markets that genuinely added value to the economy. Enron's trading operations helped stabilize energy prices and improved efficiency in power generation and distribution.

But the same financial sophistication that made Enron successful also enabled increasingly complex forms of fraud and self-deception. The company began creating elaborate off-balance-sheet partnerships to hide debt and inflate profits. These structures were so complicated that even sophisticated investors couldn't understand them, which was precisely the point. Complexity became a tool for obscuring financial reality from regulators, investors, and eventually from Enron's own executives.

The collapse, when it came, was breathtakingly rapid. Enron went from being worth $70 billion to filing for bankruptcy in less than six months, wiping out the retirement savings of thousands of employees and causing massive losses for investors. The company that had been praised for its financial innovation turned out to be an elaborate Ponzi scheme that had been stealing from its own employees and shareholders.

What makes Enron's story particularly tragic is that the company's core business model was actually sound. Energy trading did create genuine value, and many of Enron's innovations have become standard practices in commodity markets. But the pressure to maintain rapid growth led executives to supplement real profits with fictional ones, ultimately destroying a genuinely valuable business.

Lehman Brothers' collapse in 2008 followed a similar pattern of institutional arrogance leading to systemic risk-taking that eventually became unsustainable. Lehman had survived the Civil War, two World Wars, the Great Depression, and numerous financial crises over its 158-year history. The firm's executives believed their experience and expertise made them immune to the kind of risks that destroyed other investment banks.

This confidence led Lehman to take increasingly large positions in mortgage-backed securities and real estate investments, believing they could predict and manage risks that other firms couldn't handle. The strategy worked brilliantly for several years, generating record profits and establishing Lehman as one of Wall Street's most successful firms. The problem was that their risk models were based on historical data that didn't account for the possibility of a nationwide decline in real estate prices.

When the housing bubble finally burst, Lehman discovered that their sophisticated risk management systems had been measuring the wrong variables. They had calculated the probability of individual mortgage defaults with great precision, but they hadn't considered the possibility that mortgage defaults might be correlated across geographic regions and market segments. Their models assumed that real estate was a safe investment because real estate had always been a safe investment.

The resulting losses were so large that they threatened not just Lehman Brothers, but the entire global financial system. The firm that had been "too big to fail" turned out to be too big to save, requiring a government bailout that cost taxpayers hundreds of billions of dollars. The company's 158-year history ended because executives confused historical precedent with guaranteed future performance.

Both Enron and Lehman Brothers illustrate how success can become a trap for large organizations. The strategies and assumptions that made these companies successful in the short term created overconfidence that prevented them from recognizing when market conditions had changed. They became victims of their own expertise, unable to imagine that their sophisticated understanding of their industries might be based on outdated assumptions.

3. Ads That Destroyed Brands

Sometimes a single advertisement can undo decades of brand building and customer loyalty, usually because someone approved a campaign that seemed clever in the conference room but revealed tone-deaf insensitivity when exposed to the real world. These marketing disasters typically follow a predictable pattern: executives become so focused on being memorable or edgy that they lose sight of how their message might be interpreted by people outside their corporate bubble.

Pepsi's 2017 advertisement featuring Kendall Jenner became a masterclass in how to alienate your entire customer base with a single commercial. The ad depicted Jenner leaving a modeling shoot to join a street protest, ultimately defusing tensions between protesters and police by offering a Pepsi to a uniformed officer. The gesture was apparently intended to suggest that Pepsi could bring people together across social and political divisions.

The backlash was immediate and devastating. Critics pointed out that the ad trivialized real social justice movements by suggesting that police brutality and systemic racism could be solved with soft drinks and celebrity gestures. The commercial seemed to reduce genuine political protest to a fashion statement, with serious social issues serving as backdrop for product placement.

What made the controversy particularly damaging was that it revealed how disconnected Pepsi's marketing team had become from their own customers. The ad was clearly created by people who had never participated in actual political protests and had no understanding of why people might find it offensive to suggest that cola could solve complex social problems. The campaign had to be pulled within 24 hours, but the damage to Pepsi's brand reputation lasted much longer.

The Kendall Jenner ad illustrates a common problem in corporate marketing: the tendency to treat serious social issues as opportunities for brand positioning rather than genuine human concerns. Companies want to appear socially conscious and politically engaged, but they often approach these topics with a superficiality that backfires spectacularly.

United Airlines faced a similar crisis in 2017, though their problem wasn't a poorly conceived advertisement but rather a poorly handled public relations disaster that revealed the company's true priorities. When a United flight was overbooked, airline staff decided to remove passengers who had already boarded to make room for crew members who needed to reach another destination. When one passenger refused to give up his seat, he was forcibly dragged off the plane by airport security.

The incident was captured on video by other passengers and went viral within hours, showing a paying customer being physically assaulted for the crime of expecting to use the seat he had purchased. United's initial response made the situation worse by defending their employees' actions and describing the passenger as "disruptive" and "belligerent" for refusing to voluntarily give up his seat.

The company's tone-deaf response revealed a corporate culture that prioritized operational convenience over customer service. United executives seemed genuinely surprised that people were upset about a passenger being violently removed from a flight he had legally boarded. Their initial statements suggested they viewed customers as obstacles to efficient operations rather than the reason those operations existed in the first place.

The incident cost United hundreds of millions of dollars in lost bookings and required a complete overhaul of their customer service policies. But the deeper damage was to the company's reputation—the video became a symbol of corporate arrogance and indifference to customer welfare. United discovered that in the age of social media, every customer interaction is potentially a public relations crisis.

What both the Pepsi ad and the United Airlines incident reveal is how quickly corporate misjudgments can be amplified and spread through social media platforms. Companies that might have weathered similar controversies in previous decades now find that single mistakes can generate global outrage within hours. The speed and scale of modern communication make corporate tone-deafness much more dangerous than it used to be.

4. When Greed Blinded Logic

The mortgage crisis of 2008 provides a perfect case study in how short-term profit incentives can lead entire industries to ignore obvious warning signs and pursue strategies that are virtually guaranteed to end in disaster. The housing bubble wasn't caused by a single company making bad decisions—it was the result of systematic incentive structures that rewarded dangerous behavior and punished prudent risk management.

The basic problem was that mortgage lenders could generate immediate profits by issuing loans, then sell those loans to investment banks who packaged them into securities. This process, known as securitization, was supposed to reduce risk by spreading it across many investors. In practice, it created a system where nobody had incentives to care whether borrowers could actually repay their loans.

Mortgage brokers were paid based on the volume and value of loans they originated, regardless of whether those loans were likely to be repaid. Banks earned fees for processing and packaging mortgages, then sold them to other institutions before defaults became apparent. Investment banks earned fees for creating and selling mortgage-backed securities, with their profits depending on the volume of securities sold rather than their long-term performance.

Rating agencies, whose job was to assess the safety of these securities, were paid by the investment banks that created them. This created an obvious conflict of interest: agencies that gave low ratings to mortgage securities would lose business to competitors willing to provide more optimistic assessments. The result was a systematic inflation of credit ratings that bore no relationship to actual risk levels.

The entire system was designed to generate short-term profits while pushing long-term risks onto other parties. Everyone involved understood that housing prices couldn't rise indefinitely and that many subprime borrowers would eventually default on their loans. But each participant had incentives to continue the process as long as possible, hoping to profit before the inevitable collapse.

What made the situation even more dangerous was that many of the financial instruments used to package and trade mortgage risk were so complex that even sophisticated investors couldn't understand them. Collateralized debt obligations (CDOs) and synthetic CDOs created layers of abstraction between the underlying mortgages and the final investors, making it nearly impossible to assess actual risk levels.

When the housing bubble finally burst, the losses cascaded through the entire financial system because nobody had accurate information about where the risks were concentrated. Banks that thought they had diversified their mortgage exposure discovered they were actually holding multiple layers of the same underlying risks through different financial instruments.

The cryptocurrency boom and bust cycles of recent years have followed a remarkably similar pattern, with speculative investment driven more by fear of missing out than by fundamental analysis of value or utility. During the peak of cryptocurrency mania in 2017 and again in 2021, investors poured money into digital assets they didn't understand, based on promises of revolutionary technology that remained largely theoretical.

The psychology driving cryptocurrency speculation was identical to that of the housing bubble: people observed others getting rich quickly and concluded that traditional investment analysis no longer applied. The complexity of blockchain technology served the same function as complex mortgage securities—it provided a plausible-sounding explanation for why normal rules of risk and return had been suspended.

Celebrity endorsements and social media promotion amplified the speculative frenzy, with influencers and athletes promoting various cryptocurrencies to their followers without disclosing their financial interests or understanding the risks involved. The result was a series of boom and bust cycles that wiped out billions of dollars in wealth while enriching early adopters and industry insiders.

What both the mortgage crisis and cryptocurrency speculation reveal is how market bubbles develop when short-term incentives overwhelm long-term thinking. Participants know the situation is unsustainable, but they continue participating because the immediate profits seem too lucrative to ignore. The rational response for any individual is to keep playing until the music stops, even though everyone knows the music will eventually stop.

5. Business Mistakes the Whole World Laughed At

Sometimes corporate failures achieve a level of absurdity so complete that they transcend mere business mistakes and become cultural phenomena. These aren't just companies that lost money or made poor strategic decisions—they're organizations that managed to violate basic common sense so thoroughly that their failures became entertainment for everyone else.

Theranos represents perhaps the most spectacular example of corporate delusion in recent history. Elizabeth Holmes claimed to have revolutionized blood testing by developing technology that could run hundreds of tests from a single drop of blood. The claim was medically implausible—blood tests require specific volumes of blood to generate accurate results, and miniaturizing the process beyond certain limits makes reliable testing impossible.

But Holmes was so convincing in her presentations that she attracted billions of dollars in investment from sophisticated venture capitalists, built partnerships with major pharmacy chains, and achieved a company valuation of $9 billion at its peak. The technology never worked, but the company spent years faking demonstrations and manipulating test results to maintain the illusion of scientific breakthrough.

The fraud was maintained through a combination of secrecy, intimidation, and exploitation of investors' technical ignorance. Holmes claimed that revealing details about her technology would compromise competitive advantages, so investors and board members were never allowed to see actual demonstrations or review technical specifications. Employees who questioned the technology were fired or threatened with lawsuits.

When journalists finally investigated Theranos's claims, they discovered that the company was using conventional blood testing equipment for most of its tests, and that the results from their proprietary devices were so inaccurate as to be dangerous for patient care. The entire enterprise was revealed to be an elaborate con game that had somehow convinced some of America's most successful investors and business leaders.

What made the Theranos scandal particularly embarrassing for the investors involved was that the fraud could have been detected through basic technical due diligence. Any qualified medical professional could have explained why Holmes's claims were impossible, but the investors were so impressed by her Stanford credentials and compelling presentation style that they never bothered to consult actual experts.

The Fyre Festival represents a different type of corporate delusion—the belief that effective marketing can substitute for basic competence in event planning. Billy McFarland and his team promoted a luxury music festival in the Bahamas, using social media influencers and elaborate marketing campaigns to sell tickets costing thousands of dollars for what was supposed to be an exclusive experience on a private island.

The marketing was genuinely impressive, creating a sense of exclusivity and luxury that convinced thousands of wealthy young people to purchase tickets and travel to the Bahamas for the event. The problem was that McFarland had spent virtually all of his budget on marketing and celebrity endorsements, leaving almost nothing for actual festival infrastructure.

When attendees arrived, they discovered that the "luxury accommodations" were actually disaster relief tents, the "gourmet meals" were cheese sandwiches, and most of the musical acts had never been booked. The festival infrastructure was so inadequate that basic services like water and sanitation were unavailable, creating potentially dangerous conditions for attendees.

The disaster was documented in real-time through social media, with attendees posting photos and videos that showed the gap between promised luxury and actual conditions. The contrast between the polished marketing materials and the chaotic reality became a viral phenomenon, generating worldwide mockery of both the organizers and the attendees who had been gullible enough to believe the promises.

What made the Fyre Festival particularly ridiculous was that McFarland seemed genuinely surprised when his lack of planning resulted in disaster. He had apparently convinced himself that enthusiasm and marketing could overcome logistical realities, as if adequate infrastructure would somehow materialize through positive thinking and social media buzz.

Both Theranos and Fyre Festival illustrate how modern marketing and social media can create temporary realities that have no connection to actual capabilities or resources. The same tools that enable legitimate businesses to reach customers and communicate value can also enable elaborate frauds that exploit people's trust and desire to be part of something exclusive or revolutionary.

Chapter 6: The Dumbest Laws Ever Made

Human beings have been creating laws for thousands of years, which has given us plenty of time to perfect the art of legislative stupidity. The most impressive examples don't just regulate behavior in unreasonable ways—they create legal frameworks so divorced from reality that compliance becomes either impossible or absurd. These laws reveal something profound about human nature: our tendency to believe that complex social problems can be solved through sufficiently detailed regulations, regardless of whether those regulations have any connection to how the world actually works.

The pattern is always the same: legislators identify a problem (real or imagined), craft a legal solution that sounds reasonable in theory, then watch in bewilderment as the law creates new problems that are worse than whatever it was supposed to fix. The most spectacular legislative failures occur when lawmakers become so focused on the theoretical elegance of their solutions that they forget to consider how those solutions will interact with human behavior, economic incentives, and basic physics.

1. Laws That Banned Happiness

The Puritans of colonial New England achieved remarkable success in creating a legal system designed to eliminate joy from human existence. Their laws didn't just prohibit specific activities—they attempted to regulate the very concept of pleasure, as if happiness itself were a threat to social order that could be legislated out of existence through sufficiently comprehensive restrictions.

Christmas was banned in Massachusetts from 1659 to 1681 because the Puritans considered it a pagan celebration that distracted people from proper religious observance. The law imposed fines on anyone caught "observing any such day as Christmas," which included not just public celebrations but private family gatherings and even the preparation of special foods. Puritan authorities apparently believed that preventing people from celebrating the birth of Christ was the best way to honor Christian values.

The anti-Christmas law created the peculiar situation where Massachusetts residents had to pretend that December 25th was an ordinary day, even though everyone knew it wasn't. Families developed elaborate strategies for celebrating quietly, while authorities conducted inspections to ensure that nobody was enjoying themselves inappropriately. The result was a society where Christmas became a clandestine activity, like gambling or smuggling.

Dancing was similarly prohibited under laws that treated rhythmic movement as inherently sinful. The Puritan legal code didn't distinguish between different types of dancing—formal ballroom dancing, folk celebrations, and even children's games that involved coordinated movement were all considered equally dangerous to moral development. The law recognized no exceptions for weddings, community celebrations, or religious ceremonies.

Enforcement of anti-dancing laws created situations that would have been comedy gold if they weren't ruining people's lives. Town officials were required to monitor community gatherings to ensure that nobody's foot movements became too coordinated or rhythmic. Weddings were particularly problematic because traditional celebrations naturally involved music and movement, forcing couples to choose between legal compliance and cultural tradition.

The Puritans also attempted to regulate clothing choices through sumptuary laws that prohibited "excessive" decoration or luxury in dress. These laws didn't just ban specific items—they tried to control the very concept of personal adornment, as if the urge to look attractive could be eliminated through legal prohibition. Different social classes were assigned different maximum levels of clothing quality, with violations punishable by fines and public humiliation.

What made these laws particularly absurd was their attempt to regulate internal states of mind through external behavioral controls. The Puritans believed that preventing people from engaging in pleasurable activities would somehow make them more virtuous, as if morality could be imposed through legislative force rather than developed through personal choice and reflection.

The long-term effect of these happiness-prohibiting laws was to create a culture of hypocrisy where people learned to hide their natural impulses rather than examine or moderate them. Instead of fostering genuine spiritual development, the laws encouraged deception and resentment, teaching people that pleasure was inherently shameful rather than something to be enjoyed responsibly.

2. Ridiculous Rules from the USA and Beyond

American lawmakers have demonstrated remarkable creativity in crafting regulations that solve non-existent problems while creating genuine inconvenience for law-abiding citizens. These laws typically emerge from isolated incidents that trigger legislative overreaction, resulting in permanent restrictions on activities that pose no realistic threat to public safety or social order.

In Alabama, it's illegal to carry an ice cream cone in your back pocket on Sundays. This law apparently originated from concerns about horse theft—criminals supposedly used ice cream cones to lure horses away from their owners, making the theft technically legal since the horse "followed" them voluntarily. The law was presumably designed to close this loophole by making the lure itself illegal.

The horse-theft theory explains the law's existence but raises questions about the legislators' understanding of both criminal behavior and animal psychology. Horse thieves clever enough to exploit legal technicalities about animal consent probably wouldn't be deterred by ice cream cone regulations. Meanwhile, law-abiding citizens who happen to purchase frozen desserts on Sundays now face criminal liability for putting them in the wrong pocket.

In Louisiana, it's illegal to gargle in public places, though the specific definition of "public" and the acceptable volume levels for private gargling remain undefined. The law creates the bizarre situation where people with throat problems might face arrest for attempting to relieve their symptoms in ways that don't disturb anyone else. It also raises enforcement questions: do police officers receive training in distinguishing illegal gargling from legal throat clearing?.

Oklahoma has made it illegal to take a bite out of another person's hamburger, which seems like the kind of problem that would be better addressed through social etiquette than criminal law. The statute doesn't specify whether consent makes the activity legal, or whether the law applies to other sandwiches, creating potential constitutional issues around selective enforcement of food-sharing regulations.

International examples of legislative overreach can be even more spectacular. In Switzerland, it's illegal to flush the toilet after 10 PM in apartment buildings because the noise might disturb neighbors. This law forces residents to choose between basic sanitation and legal compliance, creating public health risks in service of noise control that could be better addressed through building codes or neighbor negotiations.

The Swiss toilet law illustrates a common problem in legislative problem-solving: the tendency to address symptoms rather than underlying causes. Instead of requiring better soundproofing in apartments or establishing reasonable noise ordinances, lawmakers chose to regulate bathroom usage, creating a law that's simultaneously intrusive and ineffective.

In Canada, it's illegal to pay for purchases entirely in coins if the value exceeds certain limits—$5 for nickels, $10 for dimes, and $40 for toonies. While this law was presumably designed to prevent people from making large purchases with wheelbarrows full of pennies, it also means that someone who wins a large prize from a coin-counting machine might be legally prohibited from spending their winnings.

What all these laws reveal is the legislative tendency to craft permanent solutions to temporary problems without considering long-term consequences or practical enforcement issues. A single incident of horse theft via ice cream cone becomes grounds for eternal regulation of frozen dessert transportation. One noisy late-night toilet flush becomes justification for permanently restricting bathroom usage. The cure ends up being more problematic than the disease.

3. When Politicians Tried to Regulate Nature

Some of the most spectacularly unsuccessful laws in history have been those that attempted to control natural phenomena through legislative decree, as if the physical world could be compelled to obey human political authority. These laws reveal a particular type of hubris: the belief that nature operates according to the same principles as human institutions and can therefore be regulated through similar mechanisms.

The Indiana Pi Bill of 1897 represents perhaps the purest example of legislative overreach into mathematical reality. State Representative Taylor I. Record introduced a bill that would have legally established the value of pi as exactly 3.2, based on his interpretation of Biblical passages and his conviction that the traditional value of approximately 3.14159 was unnecessarily complicated.

Record's bill wasn't just mathematically wrong—it was mathematically impossible. Pi is a fundamental mathematical constant that describes the relationship between a circle's circumference and its diameter. Changing its legal value wouldn't affect the actual mathematical relationship; it would just make all engineering and scientific calculations performed in Indiana incorrect.

The bill passed the Indiana House of Representatives by a vote of 67-0, suggesting that state legislators were either completely ignorant of basic mathematics or assumed that mathematical constants were matters of political opinion rather than objective reality. Fortunately, the bill was defeated in the state Senate after mathematics professors from Purdue University explained why legislating mathematical values was both impossible and absurd.

The Indiana Pi Bill illustrates the dangers of legislative confidence untempered by technical knowledge. The representatives who voted for the bill weren't malicious—they genuinely believed they were simplifying mathematics for the benefit of Indiana students and engineers. Their error was assuming that mathematical complexity was a political problem that could be solved through legislative action rather than an inherent feature of mathematical reality.

Even more ambitious was the King Canute law, though this one is more legendary than historical. According to popular legend, King Canute of England attempted to demonstrate his power by commanding the tide to stop rising. When the tide ignored his royal decree and continued to rise as scheduled, Canute was forced to acknowledge that natural phenomena don't respond to political authority.

The actual historical Canute was apparently trying to demonstrate the limits of royal power rather than assert control over nature, but the legend persists because it perfectly captures the absurdity of attempting to regulate natural processes through political decree. Tides, mathematical constants, and physical laws operate according to principles that are completely independent of human authority.

More recently, the Tennessee legislature attempted to regulate evolution by passing laws requiring schools to present "alternative theories" to Darwinian evolution, including theories based on religious doctrine rather than scientific evidence. While these laws don't directly contradict evolutionary processes, they attempt to control how natural history is understood and taught, as if scientific theories were matters of political preference.

The evolution laws reflect the same fundamental misunderstanding as the Indiana Pi Bill: the belief that complex natural phenomena can be simplified or modified through legislative action. Evolution isn't a political theory that can be adopted or rejected based on popular preference—it's a scientific description of observable natural processes that operate independently of human opinion.

What all these nature-regulating laws reveal is the human tendency to extend political thinking into domains where it doesn't apply. Politicians are accustomed to solving problems through negotiation, compromise, and authoritative decree. When confronted with natural phenomena that can't be negotiated with or commanded to behave differently, some lawmakers apparently conclude that the problem is insufficient legislative authority rather than inappropriate application of political solutions.

4. Legal Nonsense That Still Exists

Many of the world's most absurd laws remain officially in effect, creating potential legal liability for activities that most people consider completely harmless. These zombie regulations persist because removing outdated laws requires legislative effort that politicians prefer to spend on more visible projects, leaving legal codes cluttered with prohibitions that no longer serve any practical purpose.

In the city of York, England, it remains technically legal to shoot a Scotsman with a bow and arrow within the ancient city walls, provided the shooting occurs after midnight and the Scotsman is carrying a sword. This law apparently dates to medieval border conflicts and was never formally repealed, creating the theoretical possibility that homicide could be legal under very specific circumstances.

The York law illustrates the problem with legal systems that accumulate regulations over centuries without systematic review and revision. Medieval laws designed for medieval problems remain embedded in modern legal codes, creating bizarre exceptions to contemporary criminal statutes that nobody intended to preserve.

In London, it's illegal to die in the Houses of Parliament, though the practical enforcement mechanisms for this law remain unclear. Anyone who violates this statute would presumably be beyond the reach of criminal prosecution, making it perhaps the only law that's impossible to punish violation of. The regulation apparently exists because people who die in Parliament are technically entitled to state funerals, which the government prefers to avoid.

The no-dying law reflects the legislative tendency to solve administrative problems through criminal prohibition rather than policy clarification. Instead of simply changing the rules about state funeral entitlements, Parliament chose to make death itself illegal in certain locations, creating a law that's simultaneously unenforceable and nonsensical.

In Wales, it's illegal to enter a pub if you're drunk, which creates the logical problem of distinguishing between permissible social drinking and illegal intoxication. The law effectively makes it illegal to achieve the primary purpose for which many people visit pubs, while providing no clear guidelines for determining when someone has crossed the line from legal sobriety to criminal intoxication.

American cities have their own collections of zombie regulations that create potential legal hazards for unsuspecting citizens. In New York City, it's illegal to let your dog sleep in a bathtub, though the original purpose of this law is lost to history. Pet owners who allow their dogs to nap in dry bathtubs are technically criminals, even though the activity poses no obvious threat to public safety or animal welfare.

In San Francisco, it's illegal to wipe your car with used underwear, creating criminal liability for an activity that most people would never consider attempting anyway. The law presumably originated from a specific incident involving inappropriate cleaning materials, but it now permanently restricts automotive maintenance choices for all city residents.

What makes these persistent legal absurdities particularly problematic is that they undermine respect for law in general. When legal codes contain numerous regulations that are obviously ridiculous, it becomes harder for citizens to take the entire legal system seriously. People begin to assume that laws are arbitrary rather than rational, which reduces voluntary compliance with regulations that actually serve important purposes.

The solution would be systematic legal code review and revision, but this requires legislative time and energy that politicians prefer to spend on more politically visible activities. Cleaning up old laws doesn't generate campaign contributions or media attention, so zombie regulations persist indefinitely, cluttering legal codes with obsolete prohibitions that serve no contemporary purpose.

5. Bureaucratic Absurdities of Everyday Life

Modern bureaucracy has elevated regulatory absurdity to an art form, creating systems so complex and internally contradictory that compliance becomes impossible even for people with good intentions and legal expertise. These aren't laws designed to prohibit specific activities—they're regulatory frameworks so elaborate that they prohibit everything while providing no clear guidance on how to avoid violation.

The Americans with Disabilities Act (ADA) provides a perfect example of well-intentioned regulation that has created a labyrinth of contradictory requirements. The law requires businesses to provide "reasonable accommodation" for disabled customers and employees, but it doesn't define what constitutes "reasonable" in specific situations, leaving business owners to guess what compliance requires.

ADA compliance has generated thousands of lawsuits over issues like whether doorway widths of 31 inches versus 32 inches constitute discrimination, or whether businesses are required to provide sign language interpreters for deaf customers in all situations or only some situations. The law's vague language means that business owners can face legal liability for decisions they made in good faith based on their understanding of regulatory requirements.

The complexity is compounded by the fact that ADA requirements often conflict with other regulatory mandates. Fire codes might require door widths that conflict with disability access requirements. Zoning laws might prohibit the ramps or elevators needed for wheelchair access. Business owners can find themselves facing simultaneous violations of multiple regulations, with no clear way to achieve compliance with all applicable laws.

Tax law represents an even more spectacular example of regulatory complexity that has outgrown human comprehension. The U.S. tax code contains over 70,000 pages of regulations, exceptions, and clarifications that no individual can fully understand. Professional tax preparers regularly disagree about how specific situations should be handled, yet citizens are legally required to comply with rules that experts can't interpret consistently.

The tax code's complexity creates situations where identical economic transactions can result in completely different tax obligations depending on technical details that have no relationship to the underlying economic activity. Whether income is classified as wages, capital gains, or business profits can dramatically affect tax liability, but the classification rules are so complex that even tax professionals often disagree about which category applies.

Environmental regulations have created similar labyrinths of contradictory requirements that make compliance nearly impossible for businesses that operate in multiple jurisdictions. A single construction project might need permits from federal, state, and local agencies, each with different and sometimes contradictory requirements for environmental impact assessment and mitigation.

The permitting process can take years and cost millions of dollars, even for projects that pose no realistic environmental threat. Businesses often find that the regulatory compliance costs exceed the economic value of the projects they're trying to complete, effectively prohibiting activities that would be beneficial for both the economy and the environment.

What all these bureaucratic absurdities reveal is the fundamental problem with regulatory systems that grow through accumulation rather than design. Each new law or regulation is crafted to address a specific problem without considering how it will interact with existing requirements. Over time, the system becomes so complex that compliance becomes a matter of luck rather than intention.

The solution would require comprehensive regulatory reform and simplification, but this is politically difficult because every regulation has constituencies who benefit from its existence. Lawyers, consultants, and compliance specialists have economic interests in maintaining complex regulatory systems, while politicians prefer to add new regulations rather than simplify existing ones. The result is a legal system that grows increasingly disconnected from its original purposes.

Chapter 7: Social Media Gone Wrong

Social media promised to democratize communication, connect people across geographic boundaries, and create new opportunities for creative expression and economic development. In practice, it has also created unprecedented opportunities for spectacular public humiliation, financial disaster, and the rapid spread of dangerous misinformation. The platform that was supposed to give everyone a voice has also given everyone the ability to destroy their lives with a few poorly chosen words.

The fundamental problem with social media isn't technical—the platforms work exactly as designed. The problem is that they amplify human weaknesses that were previously contained by the practical limitations of pre-digital communication. When spreading gossip required face-to-face conversation, natural social constraints limited how quickly rumors could propagate. When expressing anger required writing letters or making phone calls, the effort involved provided time for reflection and reconsideration.

1. Tweets That Cost Millions

Elon Musk's "funding secured" tweet in August 2018 represents perhaps the most expensive social media post in history, ultimately costing him $20 million in SEC fines and his position as Tesla's chairman. The tweet claimed that Musk was considering taking Tesla private at $420 per share and that funding for the transaction was "secured." Tesla's stock price immediately jumped, suggesting that investors believed the transaction was imminent.

The problem was that funding wasn't actually secured. Musk had discussed the possibility of a buyout with Saudi investors, but no formal agreement existed, no specific terms had been negotiated, and no financing arrangements had been completed. The tweet was based on Musk's optimistic interpretation of preliminary conversations rather than actual contractual commitments.

The Securities and Exchange Commission investigation revealed that Musk had apparently chosen the $420 price partly because he thought the number would be amusing to his girlfriend—420 being slang for marijuana consumption. This meant that Musk had manipulated Tesla's stock price as part of an inside joke, causing massive financial movements based on drug humor rather than business fundamentals.

What made the incident particularly damaging was that it revealed Musk's casual attitude toward regulatory compliance and fiduciary responsibility. As

CEO of a publicly traded company, his public statements about business developments have immediate financial consequences for shareholders. Using social media to make jokes about stock prices demonstrated a fundamental misunderstanding of his legal and ethical obligations.

The "funding secured" case illustrates how social media has compressed the time between thought and communication in ways that can have catastrophic consequences for public figures. In the pre-Twitter era, corporate announcements went through legal review processes that would have caught the problems with Musk's statement. Social media platforms encourage immediate, unfiltered communication that bypasses normal institutional safeguards.

President Trump's Twitter account created even more spectacular examples of how social media posts can have massive financial and political consequences. A single tweet criticizing a specific company could immediately wipe billions of dollars off its market value, while tweets about foreign policy could destabilize international relationships and affect global financial markets.

Trump's attack on Amazon in April 2018, claiming the company was costing the Post Office "massive amounts of money," caused Amazon's stock price to drop by more than 5% in a single day, destroying over $50 billion in market value. The tweet was factually incorrect—Amazon actually generates profits for the Post Office through its shipping partnerships—but the market responded to the presidential criticism before fact-checkers could provide clarification.

The Amazon case demonstrates how social media has given individual users, even powerful ones, the ability to cause massive economic disruption through unverified claims. Traditional media outlets would have fact-checked claims about corporate financial relationships before publishing them, but social media platforms provide no editorial oversight or verification processes.

2. Celebrity Posts That Backfired Spectacularly

Kim Kardashian's promotion of EthereumMax cryptocurrency in June 2021 demonstrates how celebrity endorsements on social media can lead to both legal and financial disaster. Kardashian posted an Instagram story encouraging her 250 million followers to buy EMAX tokens, describing the cryptocurrency as a promising investment opportunity without disclosing that she was being paid for the promotion.

The post generated massive buying activity that drove up EMAX prices temporarily, but the value collapsed within days as investors realized the cryptocurrency had no practical utility or sustainable business model. Many of Kardashian's followers lost substantial money on investments they made based on her recommendation, while early investors and insiders profited from the temporary price spike.

The Securities and Exchange Commission later fined Kardashian $1.26 million for failing to disclose her paid partnership with EthereumMax, but the financial damage to her followers was much larger. The incident revealed how social media influencers can inadvertently facilitate financial fraud by promoting investments they don't understand to audiences who trust their recommendations.

What made Kardashian's cryptocurrency promotion particularly problematic was that she presented investment advice as casual social sharing. The Instagram post looked like personal enthusiasm for a new financial product rather than paid advertising for a speculative investment. This blurred the line between authentic personal communication and commercial promotion in ways that deceived her audience.

Logan Paul's "suicide forest" video in December 2017 created a different type of celebrity social media disaster, one that damaged his reputation and forced major platforms to reconsider their content policies. Paul posted a YouTube video showing a dead body in Japan's Aokigahara forest, an area known for high suicide rates. The video was intended as dark humor but was widely criticized as exploitative and insensitive.

The backlash was immediate and severe. YouTube suspended Paul from its advertising program, causing him to lose millions of dollars in potential revenue. Major brands ended sponsorship deals, and other content creators distanced themselves from association with his channel. The incident demonstrated how quickly social media success can turn into career-ending scandal.

Paul's response to the controversy made the situation worse. Instead of immediately apologizing and removing the content, he initially defended the video as raising awareness about suicide prevention. This tone-deaf response extended the controversy and amplified criticism from mental health advocates, other YouTubers, and mainstream media outlets.

The suicide forest incident illustrates how social media platforms reward sensational content without providing adequate guardrails for ethical decision-making. Paul's video was designed to generate views and engagement, which translated directly into advertising revenue. The platform's algorithms promoted controversial content without considering its potential social harm.

What both the Kardashian cryptocurrency promotion and Paul's suicide forest video reveal is how social media has created new categories of public irresponsibility. Traditional celebrities worked within institutional frameworks that provided some oversight and guidance for public statements and creative content. Social media influencers operate with minimal institutional support but maximum potential for both positive and negative impact.

3. Internet Sleuths Who Got It Completely Wrong

The Boston Marathon bombing investigation of 2013 became a case study in how social media crowdsourcing can amplify misinformation and obstruct legitimate law enforcement efforts. Within hours of the bombing, Reddit users created forums dedicated to identifying the perpetrators by analyzing photographs and videos from the scene. The project seemed like a positive use of distributed intelligence and civic engagement.

The crowdsourced investigation quickly focused on Sunil Tripathi, a Brown University student who had been missing for weeks before the bombing. Reddit users convinced themselves that Tripathi matched the physical description of one suspect and began circulating his photo as a wanted terrorist. The identification spread across social media platforms, with thousands of users sharing Tripathi's image and personal information.

The problem was that Tripathi had nothing to do with the bombing. He had committed suicide before the attack occurred, though his body wasn't discovered until after the false identification had spread globally. Meanwhile, the actual perpetrators remained free while law enforcement resources were diverted to investigate the wrong suspects.

The false identification had devastating consequences for Tripathi's family, who received death threats and harassment from people convinced they were protecting terrorists. The family was forced to leave their home and hire security while mourning their son's suicide and dealing with his posthumous vilification as a terrorist.

The Reddit investigation illustrates the fundamental problems with crowdsourced criminal investigations. Professional investigators follow systematic procedures designed to prevent false identifications and protect innocent people from wrongful accusation. Amateur internet sleuths operate without training, oversight, or accountability, making them prone to exactly the kind of errors that occurred in the Boston case.

The Pizzagate conspiracy theory of 2016 represents an even more dangerous example of internet investigation gone wrong. Social media users convinced themselves that a Washington D.C. pizza restaurant was the center of a child trafficking ring involving prominent politicians. The theory was based entirely on creative misinterpretation of Democratic Party emails leaked during the election campaign.

The conspiracy theory spread rapidly through social media platforms, with users sharing "evidence" that consisted of normal business communications interpreted through the assumption that everything was code for illegal activities. The restaurant began receiving death threats, and employees were harassed by people demanding access to a non-existent basement where children were supposedly being held.

The situation escalated when Edgar Maddison Welch drove from North Carolina to Washington with an assault rifle to "investigate" the alleged child trafficking. Welch fired shots inside the restaurant while searching for evidence of the conspiracy, endangering staff and customers. He found no evidence because no conspiracy existed, but his armed investigation could easily have resulted in multiple deaths.

The Pizzagate incident demonstrates how internet conspiracy theories can motivate real-world violence based on completely fabricated evidence. Social media platforms amplified the conspiracy theory without fact-checking its claims, while users convinced themselves they were conducting legitimate investigations of serious crimes.

What both the Boston Marathon and Pizzagate cases reveal is how social media has democratized criminal investigation in ways that undermine both accuracy and public safety. The same tools that enable legitimate crowdsourcing and citizen journalism also enable vigilante justice based on misinformation and speculation. The platforms provide no mechanism for distinguishing between helpful citizen engagement and dangerous mob behavior.

4. Dangerous Online Trends That Ended in Hospitals

The Tide Pod challenge of 2017-2018 represents perhaps the purest example of how social media can transform obviously dangerous activities into viral entertainment. The "challenge" involved biting into laundry detergent pods and filming the reaction, despite the fact that detergent pods are designed to be toxic to prevent accidental ingestion. The trend apparently began as dark humor but evolved into actual consumption by people seeking social media attention.

Poison control centers reported a dramatic increase in calls related to detergent pod ingestion, with many cases involving teenagers who had deliberately consumed the products as part of social media challenges. The detergents caused severe chemical burns to mouth, throat, and digestive tract tissues, requiring emergency medical treatment and sometimes hospitalization.

What made the Tide Pod challenge particularly baffling was that the danger was obvious and immediate. Unlike other risky social media trends that might cause delayed or uncertain harm, eating laundry detergent produces immediate, severe, and visible injuries. Participants weren't unaware of the risks—they were pursuing social media fame despite understanding the consequences.

The challenge illustrates how social media algorithms can amplify dangerous behavior by rewarding engagement regardless of content quality or safety. Videos of people injuring themselves generated views, likes, and comments, which translated into social media attention and potential monetization opportunities. The platforms promoted harmful content because it generated user engagement.

The cinnamon challenge preceded Tide Pods as an example of viral self-harm disguised as entertainment. Participants attempted to swallow a spoonful of ground cinnamon without drinking water, then filmed their reaction as they choked, gagged, and often vomited from the experience. The challenge seemed harmless but could actually cause serious respiratory problems from inhaling cinnamon powder.

Medical professionals warned that the cinnamon challenge could cause lung inflammation, scarring, and even collapsed lungs in severe cases. The fine cinnamon powder, when inhaled, can create blockages in airways and cause chemical pneumonia. Several participants required emergency medical treatment for breathing difficulties.

The fire challenge took viral self-harm to even more extreme levels, with participants pouring flammable liquids on themselves and setting them on fire while filming the experience. This trend resulted in multiple severe burn injuries, including cases that required skin grafts and months of recovery. Some participants suffered permanent disfigurement from injuries sustained while attempting to create viral content.

What all these dangerous trends reveal is how social media has created incentive structures that reward self-destructive behavior. Traditional media outlets wouldn't broadcast footage of people deliberately injuring themselves, but social media platforms have no editorial oversight to prevent the spread of harmful content.

The viral nature of social media also means that dangerous trends can spread faster than safety warnings or medical advice. By the time health professionals and safety advocates identify a harmful trend and begin educating people about its risks, thousands of people may have already attempted the activity and injured themselves.

Platform algorithms compound the problem by promoting content that generates strong reactions, regardless of whether those reactions are positive or negative. Videos of people injuring themselves often generate both fascinated viewing and horrified commenting, which the algorithms interpret as successful content that should be shown to more users.

5. Influencers Who Lost to Their Own Hype

Belle Gibson built a massive social media following by claiming she had cured her brain cancer through diet and lifestyle changes rather than conventional medical treatment. Her Instagram account and mobile app promoted "healing" recipes and wellness advice based on her personal experience overcoming a terminal diagnosis. Gibson became a successful influencer in the wellness community, earning substantial income from sponsorships and product sales.

The problem was that Gibson had never had cancer. Her entire social media presence was built on fabricated medical history and fictional recovery story. When journalists investigated her claims, they discovered that she had no medical records supporting her cancer diagnosis and that her "healing journey" was entirely fictional.

The revelation destroyed Gibson's career and credibility, but the damage extended beyond her personal consequences. Thousands of followers had made medical decisions based on her advice, potentially delaying or avoiding conventional cancer treatments in favor of dietary approaches that had no proven effectiveness against cancer.

Gibson's case illustrates the dangerous intersection between social media influence and medical misinformation. Her fabricated story gained credibility through repetition and engagement rather than medical verification, demonstrating how social media platforms can amplify health misinformation that puts lives at risk.

James Charles, one of YouTube's most successful beauty influencers, experienced a different type of social media downfall when he became involved in public feuds with other influencers over business relationships and personal conduct. Charles built his career on makeup tutorials and product reviews, accumulating millions of subscribers and lucrative sponsorship deals.

His problems began when he promoted a competitor to a friend and mentor's vitamin company during a music festival, leading to a public dispute about business loyalty and personal relationships. The conflict escalated into accusations of inappropriate behavior with fans, creating a scandal that cost Charles millions of subscribers and numerous sponsorship deals.

The Charles controversy demonstrates how quickly influencer careers can collapse when personal relationships become public entertainment. Social media audiences often feel invested in influencers' personal lives, but this creates vulnerability when private disputes become public spectacles.

Both Gibson and Charles illustrate the fundamental instability of careers built entirely on social media presence and personal branding. Traditional celebrities work within industry structures that provide some insulation from personal scandals and professional setbacks. Social media influencers have direct relationships with their audiences that provide greater income potential but also greater vulnerability to rapid career destruction.

The influencer economy also creates incentives for increasingly extreme behavior as creators compete for attention in saturated markets. The pressure to maintain engagement and growth can lead influencers to make progressively riskier content choices or personal disclosures that eventually backfire spectacularly.

Chapter 8: The Psychology of Stupidity

After surveying centuries of human folly across every domain of human activity, certain patterns begin to emerge. The same cognitive biases, social pressures, and decision-making errors appear repeatedly, whether we're examining military disasters, scientific failures, government blunders, or corporate catastrophes. Understanding why intelligent people consistently make spectacularly bad decisions isn't just academic curiosity—it's essential for avoiding similar mistakes in our own lives.

The most important insight from studying human stupidity is that it's not primarily a problem of intelligence or education. Many of history's most spectacular failures were perpetrated by brilliant, well-educated people who had access to excellent information and strong incentives to make good decisions. The problem isn't that people lack the cognitive capacity to think clearly—it's that thinking clearly is much harder than it appears, especially when social, emotional, and institutional pressures are working against rationality.

1. Why Smart People Do Dumb Things

Intelligence, it turns out, provides surprisingly little protection against monumentally bad decision-making. In fact, highly intelligent people may be more susceptible to certain types of errors because their intellectual confidence makes them less likely to question their own reasoning or seek outside perspectives that might challenge their conclusions.

The Enron executives who destroyed one of America's largest corporations weren't stupid—they were graduates of elite business schools who understood complex financial instruments and sophisticated risk management techniques. Their failure wasn't due to lack of analytical capability, but to a combination of overconfidence, groupthink, and incentive structures that rewarded short-term results over long-term sustainability.

Jeffrey Skilling, Enron's CEO, was a Harvard MBA who had been a successful McKinsey consultant before joining the company. He genuinely believed that his innovative trading strategies would revolutionize the energy industry, and his confidence in this vision prevented him from recognizing warning signs that would have been obvious to someone with less intellectual investment in the company's approach.

The problem wasn't that Skilling lacked the intelligence to understand Enron's financial problems—it was that his intelligence had been enlisted in service of self-deception. Smart people are often better at rationalizing bad decisions than recognizing them, because they can construct more sophisticated justifications for continuing down destructive paths.

This pattern appears throughout history. The generals who led disastrous military campaigns were often highly educated professionals with extensive training and experience. The scientists who promoted dangerous theories were typically experts in their fields with impressive academic credentials. The politicians who implemented catastrophic policies were usually intelligent people who understood the complexities of governance.

What intelligence does provide is the ability to create elaborate justifications for decisions that serve emotional or social needs rather than rational analysis. Smart people can convince themselves that risky investments are actually prudent, that obviously false theories are actually sophisticated insights, or that clearly destructive policies are actually necessary reforms.

The Theranos scandal illustrates this dynamic perfectly. Elizabeth Holmes wasn't unintelligent—she was a Stanford student who understood enough about biotechnology to create convincing presentations about revolutionary medical devices. Her intelligence enabled her to construct elaborate narratives that convinced sophisticated investors, board members, and business partners to believe in technology that didn't exist.

The investors who funded Theranos weren't stupid either—they were successful venture capitalists and business leaders with extensive experience evaluating technology companies. But their intelligence worked against them by enabling them to rationalize their investment decisions with sophisticated-sounding analyses that ignored obvious red flags.

What these cases reveal is that intelligence without wisdom can actually be dangerous. Smart people who lack emotional self-awareness, social humility, or institutional constraints can cause far more damage than less intelligent people who recognize their limitations and seek advice from others.

2. The Dunning-Kruger Effect Explained Through Real Stories

The Dunning-Kruger effect describes the tendency for people with limited knowledge in a particular area to overestimate their expertise, while those with greater knowledge tend to underestimate their relative competence. This cognitive bias helps explain why confident ignorance often defeats careful expertise in public debates, political campaigns, and business decisions.

David Dunning and Justin Kruger's original research involved testing people's abilities in areas like logic, grammar, and humor, then asking them to estimate their performance relative to others. Consistently, the worst performers dramatically overestimated their abilities, rating themselves as above average despite scoring in the bottom quartile. Meanwhile, the best performers underestimated their relative skills, assuming that tasks easy for them were equally easy for everyone else.

The effect occurs because incompetent people lack the metacognitive skills needed to recognize their own incompetence. The same knowledge deficits that produce poor performance also prevent people from understanding what good performance looks like. It's a double curse: not knowing, and not knowing that you don't know.

Brexit provides a compelling real-world example of Dunning-Kruger in action. The referendum campaign revealed a stark divide between experts who understood the complexity of EU-UK relationships and voters who confidently dismissed expert warnings as "Project Fear." Many Brexit supporters genuinely believed that leaving the European Union would be simple and beneficial, despite having limited understanding of trade relationships, regulatory frameworks, or international law.

The confidence of Brexit advocates wasn't based on superior knowledge—it was based on their inability to comprehend the complexity of what they were proposing. People who understood international trade relationships recognized how difficult Brexit implementation would be, while those with limited knowledge assumed it would be straightforward.

The resulting Brexit negotiations proved the experts correct about the complexity and difficulty of the process, but by then the political decision had already been made based on confident ignorance rather than informed analysis. The Dunning-Kruger effect had enabled poorly informed public opinion to override expert knowledge with catastrophic consequences.

Donald Trump's presidential campaign and administration provided numerous examples of Dunning-Kruger effect in political leadership. Trump's confidence in his ability to solve complex problems—from Middle East peace to healthcare reform to trade negotiations—was inversely related to his actual knowledge about these issues. His certainty that simple solutions existed for complicated problems reflected classic overconfidence driven by ignorance of the domains involved.

Trump's approach to COVID-19 policy exemplified Dunning-Kruger dynamics. Despite having no medical or epidemiological training, he confidently contradicted public health experts and promoted treatments that had no scientific basis. His certainty about medical interventions he didn't understand reflected the characteristic overconfidence that comes from not knowing enough to recognize what you don't know.

The social media environment amplifies Dunning-Kruger effects by providing platforms where confident ignorance can compete directly with careful expertise without institutional filters. YouTube videos promoting conspiracy theories can reach larger audiences than peer-reviewed scientific papers, and social media algorithms often promote engaging content over accurate content.

Climate change denial illustrates how Dunning-Kruger effects can be exploited for political purposes. People with limited understanding of atmospheric physics, climate modeling, or statistical analysis can be easily convinced that they understand these topics better than professional climate scientists. Their overconfidence makes them susceptible to misinformation designed to exploit their knowledge gaps.

What all these examples reveal is that the Dunning-Kruger effect isn't just an individual psychological quirk—it's a systematic vulnerability that can be exploited to manipulate public opinion and undermine evidence-based decision-making. Recognizing the effect is the first step toward developing intellectual humility and seeking reliable expertise rather than confident ignorance.

3. How Stupidity Spreads Like a Virus

Stupidity isn't just an individual phenomenon—it's contagious. Bad ideas, false beliefs, and irrational behaviors can spread through populations with remarkable speed and efficiency, often outcompeting accurate information and rational analysis. Understanding how this happens is crucial for protecting ourselves and our institutions from intellectual epidemics.

The key insight is that stupidity spreads through social networks rather than logical analysis. People adopt beliefs and behaviors based on what their friends, colleagues, and social groups consider normal or acceptable, not based on independent evaluation of evidence. This means that false ideas with strong social support can defeat true ideas that lack social reinforcement.

The anti-vaccination movement illustrates this dynamic perfectly. The original study linking vaccines to autism was fraudulent and has been thoroughly debunked by overwhelming scientific evidence. Yet anti-vaccination beliefs have continued to spread and even grow stronger in some communities, leading to outbreaks of preventable diseases.

The persistence of anti-vaccine beliefs despite contradictory evidence occurs because these beliefs serve social functions beyond their factual content. They allow parents to demonstrate concern for their children's welfare, signal distrust of authority figures, and maintain membership in communities that share these values. The social benefits of belief persist even when the factual basis disappears.

Social media platforms have accelerated the spread of intellectual contagions by creating echo chambers where false beliefs can circulate without encountering correction or challenge. Anti-vaccine groups can share misinformation exclusively with people who already agree with them, reinforcing their confidence while avoiding exposure to contradictory evidence.

The QAnon conspiracy theory demonstrates how complex belief systems can spread like viruses through online communities. The theory involves elaborate claims about secret government operations, celebrity involvement in criminal conspiracies, and hidden messages in public communications. None of these claims are supported by credible evidence, yet millions of people have adopted QAnon beliefs.

QAnon spreads through gamification of conspiracy thinking, encouraging believers to find "clues" and "decode" messages in normal political communications. This process creates psychological investment in the belief system that makes believers resistant to contradictory evidence. The more effort people put into "researching" QAnon theories, the more committed they become to believing them.

The social media algorithms that promote engaging content have inadvertently created ideal conditions for spreading intellectual contagions. False and outrageous claims often generate more engagement than true but boring information, so platforms promote misinformation not because it's accurate but because it's psychologically compelling.

Financial bubbles represent another type of intellectual contagion, where irrational optimism spreads through investor communities and creates market behavior that contradicts fundamental economic analysis. The dot-com bubble of the late 1990s convinced millions of investors that internet companies were worth hundreds of billions of dollars despite having no profits or clear business models.

The cryptocurrency bubbles of recent years have followed similar patterns, with speculative investment driven more by fear of missing out than by rational analysis of utility or value. Social media promotion and celebrity endorsements have accelerated the spread of crypto-enthusiasm, creating massive price bubbles that eventually collapse when reality reasserts itself.

What all these examples reveal is that stupidity spreads through emotional and social mechanisms rather than logical ones. People adopt beliefs because they want to belong to certain groups, signal certain values, or avoid certain social costs. Once false beliefs become socially entrenched, they can become nearly impossible to dislodge through rational argument or evidence.

4. The Self-Destruct Mechanism in the Human Brain

Human psychology contains built-in biases and decision-making shortcuts that were adaptive for our evolutionary environment but can be catastrophically maladaptive in modern contexts. These cognitive features aren't bugs in the human operating system—they're features that helped our ancestors survive but now often lead us into disaster.

Confirmation bias, the tendency to seek information that supports existing beliefs while ignoring contradictory evidence, was probably useful when quick decisions about threats and opportunities were matters of life and death. In modern contexts, however, confirmation bias can lead people to persist in destructive behaviors long after evidence shows they're not working.

The sunk cost fallacy illustrates this problem perfectly. People continue investing time, money, and effort into failing projects because they've already invested so much that quitting feels like admitting failure. This bias probably evolved to prevent our ancestors from giving up too easily on projects that required persistence, but it now causes people to throw good money after bad in situations where cutting losses would be rational.

Corporate executives continue funding failing projects because admitting error would damage their reputations. Governments continue fighting unwinnable wars because withdrawal would appear to waste previous sacrifices. Individuals continue bad relationships or unfulfilling careers because starting over feels like abandoning their investment of time and energy.

Loss aversion, the tendency to feel losses more intensely than equivalent gains, creates similar problems in modern decision-making. People often refuse to take reasonable risks because they're more focused on what they might lose than what they might gain. This bias was probably adaptive when resources were scarce and losses could be fatal, but it now prevents people from making rational trade-offs.

The availability heuristic causes people to estimate probabilities based on how easily they can recall examples, which leads to systematic misperceptions of risk. Dramatic, memorable events like plane crashes or terrorist attacks seem more likely than they actually are, while boring, statistical risks like heart disease or car accidents are underestimated.

Media coverage amplifies availability bias by focusing attention on rare but dramatic events while ignoring common but mundane risks. People become afraid of flying while texting and driving, worried about shark attacks while ignoring swimming pool safety, or concerned about terrorism while ignoring climate change.

Social proof bias causes people to assume that popular behaviors are correct behaviors, even when the popularity isn't based on rational analysis. If everyone else is buying a particular stock, investing in a certain cryptocurrency, or following a specific diet, it must be a good idea. This bias probably helped our ancestors learn from their communities, but it now causes people to follow crowds over cliffs.

The housing bubble of the 2000s was driven largely by social proof bias. People assumed that buying houses was a good investment because everyone else was buying houses. The popularity of real estate investment created a feedback loop where rising prices seemed to validate the wisdom of buying, even though the price increases were caused by speculative behavior rather than fundamental value.

Overconfidence bias causes people to overestimate their abilities, knowledge, and chances of success. This bias probably helped our ancestors take necessary risks and project confidence in social situations, but it now causes people to attempt tasks they're not qualified for and make bets they can't afford to lose.

What makes these biases particularly dangerous is that they operate below conscious awareness. People don't choose to be overconfident or loss-averse—these tendencies are built into the basic architecture of human cognition. Recognizing them requires constant vigilance and systematic effort to counteract natural psychological tendencies.

5. Laughing at Stupidity Without Becoming Part of It

The final challenge in studying human stupidity is maintaining perspective and humility about our own susceptibility to the same errors we observe in others. It's easy to feel superior to historical figures who made obviously bad decisions or contemporary people who fall for transparent scams, but this sense of superiority is exactly the kind of overconfidence that leads to spectacular failures.

The most dangerous attitude toward human stupidity is the assumption that we're somehow immune to the same cognitive biases and social pressures that trap everyone else. This meta-stupidity—being stupid about stupidity—can lead to even worse decisions than simple ignorance or incompetence.

Carlo Cipolla, the Italian economist who developed the fundamental laws of human stupidity, identified this problem in his analysis of how intelligent people underestimate the threat posed by stupid behavior. Smart people often assume that stupid actions will have predictable consequences that can be easily avoided, but this assumption ignores the fundamental unpredictability of stupidity.

The Brexit referendum provides a perfect example of this dynamic. Many educated, well-informed people dismissed the possibility that voters would choose to leave the European Union because the economic costs seemed obviously prohibitive. Their analysis was technically correct, but it failed to account for the role of emotion, identity, and social signaling in political decision-making.

Similarly, many financial experts dismissed the possibility of a housing bubble in the 2000s because the risks seemed obvious to anyone with basic economic training. Their confidence in their own analytical abilities prevented them from recognizing that market participants weren't making decisions based on rational economic analysis.

The key to maintaining perspective is recognizing that intelligence and education provide tools for better decision-making, but they don't eliminate the fundamental human susceptibility to cognitive bias, social pressure, and emotional reasoning. Smart people can use their intelligence to construct more sophisticated rationalizations for bad decisions, making them potentially more dangerous than obviously incompetent people.

Developing intellectual humility requires acknowledging that our own reasoning is subject to the same limitations that we observe in others. This doesn't mean abandoning confidence in evidence-based thinking—it means recognizing that evidence-based thinking is harder than it appears and requires constant vigilance against our natural psychological tendencies.

The most effective protection against stupidity—both our own and others'—is building systems and institutions that are designed to counteract human cognitive limitations rather than assuming those limitations don't exist. This means creating decision-making processes that require multiple perspectives, encourage dissent, and provide mechanisms for correcting errors before they become catastrophes.

Historical examples of successful stupidity prevention often involve institutional structures that force people to confront their biases and test their assumptions. The scientific method works not because scientists are less susceptible to bias than other people, but because it creates systematic procedures for detecting and correcting errors. Democratic institutions work not because politicians are particularly wise, but because they create mechanisms for removing leaders who make consistently bad decisions.

The challenge in modern society is that many of our most important decisions—about technology, climate change, economic policy, and international relations—require expertise that most people don't possess, but also have consequences that affect everyone. This creates a tension between democratic decision-making and evidence-based analysis that has no easy resolution.

The best approach may be what philosophers call "epistemic humility"—recognizing the limits of our own knowledge while still maintaining confidence in reliable sources of expertise. This means being skeptical of confident claims while still being able to distinguish between legitimate expertise and confident ignorance.

Ultimately, the goal isn't to eliminate stupidity—that's impossible given the constraints of human psychology and social organization. The goal is to minimize its consequences by building resilient systems that can survive occasional spectacular failures and learn from inevitable mistakes. This requires accepting that stupidity is a permanent feature of the human condition while working to reduce its impact on our collective welfare.

The greatest danger may not be stupidity itself, but the arrogance that comes from believing we've transcended it. Every generation thinks it's smarter than its predecessors and immune to their mistakes, yet every generation manages to find new and creative ways to demonstrate that human folly is remarkably consistent across time and culture.

Epilogue: The Eternal Return of Human Folly

As I finish writing this catalog of human stupidity, I'm struck by a disturbing realization: someone, somewhere, is probably reading this book while making exactly the kind of spectacularly bad decision that would earn them a place in a future edition. The human capacity for creative self-destruction appears to be one of our most reliable and enduring characteristics.

The stories in this book span thousands of years and cover every domain of human activity, yet the underlying patterns remain remarkably consistent. People in ancient Rome made the same basic categories of errors as people in medieval Europe, Victorian England, or contemporary America. The technology changes, the context evolves, but the fundamental mechanisms of human folly remain depressingly constant.

This consistency suggests that stupidity isn't a bug in the human operating system—it's a feature. The same cognitive biases and social dynamics that lead to spectacular failures also enable the cooperation, risk-taking, and rapid decision-making that have made human civilization possible. Our capacity for overconfidence enables entrepreneurship and exploration. Our tendency to follow social proof enables large-scale coordination. Our susceptibility to emotional reasoning enables art, love, and moral commitment.

The challenge isn't to eliminate these tendencies—that would be like trying to redesign human nature itself. The challenge is to create systems and institutions that harness the benefits of human psychology while minimizing its destructive potential. Sometimes we succeed at this, creating markets that channel self-interest toward social benefit, democratic institutions that prevent the concentration of power, or scientific methods that systematically overcome individual bias.

But just as often, we create new opportunities for old mistakes. Social media platforms that were designed to connect people have become engines for spreading misinformation and amplifying outrage. Financial innovations that were supposed to reduce risk have created new forms of systemic instability. Communication technologies that promised to make us smarter have often made us more susceptible to manipulation and tribal thinking.

Perhaps the most sobering lesson from this survey of human folly is that intelligence, education, and good intentions provide much less protection against stupidity than we'd like to believe. Some of history's most spectacular disasters were created by brilliant people who understood their domains deeply and genuinely wanted to make the world better. The road to catastrophe is paved with PhD dissertations and Nobel Prize citations.

This doesn't mean we should abandon rationality or expertise—quite the opposite. It means we should approach both with appropriate humility and systematic safeguards against overconfidence. The people who make the worst mistakes are often those who are most certain they can't be wrong, while the people who make the fewest mistakes are often those who assume they probably are wrong about something important.

The stories in this book should serve as a mirror rather than a window—a way of examining our own susceptibility to the same errors that seem so obvious when we observe them in others. Every corporate executive who reads about Enron should ask what accounting irregularities they might be overlooking. Every government official who reads about bureaucratic disasters should wonder what unintended consequences their policies might produce. Every investor who reads about financial bubbles should consider whether they're currently caught up in one.

But perhaps most importantly, we should remember that human stupidity, while often catastrophic, is also frequently hilarious. The capacity to laugh at our own mistakes—and at the mistakes of others—may be one of our species' most valuable adaptations. Humor provides psychological distance from failure, enables learning from error, and creates social bonds that help us cooperate despite our individual limitations.

The ancient Greek concept of hubris—excessive pride that leads to downfall—assumed that the gods would punish mortals who became too confident in their own abilities. In our secular age, we don't need divine intervention to bring down the overconfident. Human stupidity provides its own punishment, with a reliability that would make any deity jealous.

So as you close this book and return to your own life, remember that you are almost certainly in the process of making mistakes that will seem obvious to future observers. The question isn't whether you'll do stupid things—it's whether you'll do them in ways that are merely embarrassing or genuinely catastrophic.

Choose your stupidity wisely. The world has enough catastrophes already, but it can always use more good stories about the eternal human capacity to snatch defeat from the jaws of victory, to solve simple problems in impossibly complicated ways, and to demonstrate that evolution has equipped us to survive as a species while remaining individually capable of the most breathtaking displays of poor judgment.

In the end, perhaps that's the most human thing about us: our unlimited creativity in finding new ways to be wrong, combined with our unlimited optimism that this time will be different. It never is, of course. But somehow, we keep trying anyway, and occasionally, despite our best efforts to mess things up, we accidentally get something right.

That might be the most encouraging thought of all: in a universe full of humans making spectacularly bad decisions, the fact that civilization exists at all suggests that our capacity for occasional wisdom might just barely outweigh our talent for creative destruction. At least until someone reads this book and decides to prove me wrong.

THE END

Printed in France by Amazon
Brétigny-sur-Orge, FR